Safeguarding India

Safeguarding India

Essays on Governance and Security

N.N. VOHRA

HarperCollins *Publishers* India

First published in hardback in India in 2016 by
HarperCollins *Publishers* India

P-ISBN: 978-93-5177-542-3
E-ISBN: 978-93-5177-543-0

2 4 6 8 10 9 7 5 3 1

HarperCollins *Publishers*
A-75, Sector 57, Noida, Uttar Pradesh 201301, India
1 London Bridge Street, London, SE1 9GF, United Kingdom
Hazelton Lanes, 55 Avenue Road, Suite 2900, Toronto, Ontario M5R 3L2
and 1995 Markham Road, Scarborough, Ontario M1B 5M8, Canada
25 Ryde Road, Pymble, Sydney, NSW 2073, Australia
195 Broadway, New York NY 10007, USA

Typeset in 11/14 Bembo Std
by Jojy Philip, New Delhi

Printed and bound at
Replika Press Pvt. Ltd.

To all the brave men in uniform, the unsung heroes,
who continue to lay down their lives for safeguarding
the country's unity and integrity.

Contents

Governance: Challenges and Opportunities

Appendixes

Preface

Not too long from now, the people of India would have basked under national governance for seven decades – not a very long time in a nation's history but a long enough period to look back and reckon whether the management of the country's affairs has been on track, and to be re-assured that we are steadily progressing towards the attainment of the crucial goals that would enable India to soon take its place among the developed nations.

Of sub-continental dimensions, India has land and sea borders running to nearly 23,000 km, about 1,200 islands and an EEZ of several million square kilometres. The country's growing population of over a billion and a quarter comprises 4,635 multi-religious communities, which speak 179 languages and nearly 550 dialects and whose vastly varying socio-cultural traditions are embedded in thousands of years of history. The management of such an intensely variegated spectrum requires the pursuit of visionary ideologies and governance which is truly rooted in social, economic and political justice.

The destinies of nations are shaped by a host of internal and external influences. And in today's growingly connected world, varied geo-political and other developments, even those which take place far beyond our frontiers, have the potential of generating worrisome security problems. This has been amply demonstrated in the recent years by the rapid spread of radical ideologies and the gruesome terror strikes in several parts of the world.

The quality of governance is the foremost among the domestic factors which influence the pace and direction of nation building. The ruling political parties can provide beneficial governance only if they are impelled by the singular objective of promoting equitable growth and development and the welfare of all the people by running an administrative system which functions with visible speed, efficiency, accountability and honesty.

Good governance also needs to ensure that peace and normalcy prevails in the realm, and the populace feels safe and secure. Against the backdrop of the growing onslaught of terrorism, the maintenance of an assured environment requires uncompromising adherence to the Constitution and rule of law, and a security management machinery which, manned by especially trained personnel, has nation-wide jurisdiction to investigate and prosecute terror and organised crime without any impediment. To deliver these objectives we require a national security management policy and a corresponding legal and administrative framework to implement it effectively.

During the course of my service, and even after my retirement, I have been involved in the management of security related challenges – along the country's frontiers, in border states and while working in the Ministry of Home Affairs. I have also had the opportunity of working with colleagues and experts to evolve courses of action for dealing with problems arising from the failures of governance and security management. It is a matter for considerable anxiety that challenges to national security, some of which surfaced decades ago, have since gathered frightening dimensions.

This volume contains a selection of my writings and lectures, which seek to draw attention to some of the problems that arise from the gaps and deficiencies in the functioning of the administrative and security systems. It is hoped that the essays in this volume shall evoke interest among the concerned authorities to evolve a clear and resolute approach for the effective management of all matters which relate to safeguarding the unity and integrity of India.

7 December 2015,   N.N.Vohra
Raj Bhavan,
Jammu.

National Security

Internal and External

1

Is India under Threat?[*]

India's prolonged struggle for independence led to tensions, confrontations and clashes among its different communities. The growing turbulence especially affected West Bengal, North-West Frontier Province (NWFP), Sindh and Punjab, resulting in riot, arson and the killing of hundreds of thousands of people. Law and order was seriously disturbed and remained so even after 15 August 1947.

India's first home minister, Vallabhbhai Patel, was an experienced, astute and far-sighted leader. Imbued with a clear vision and determination, he was able to restore normalcy to the disturbed areas. At that time, the Ministry of Home Affairs (MHA) was responsible for the maintenance of public order, the operation of public services (which comprised the all-India and Central services) and the governance of the centrally administered areas. The equation between the provincial chief ministers and the Central leadership compounded with the home ministry's effective control over the services enabled it to exercise meaningful influence over the administration of the country. Undoubtedly, this was an important factor in the maintenance of law and order. The effective functioning of the Centre also enabled the country to successfully thwart the Pakistan-organized invasion of the Kashmir Valley earlier in the winter of 1947.

---

[*] First published in *World Affairs*, Vol. 1, No. 3, July–September 1997.

CONSTITUTIONAL STIPULATIONS REGARDING SECURITY

In the division of responsibility between the Union and the states under the Indian Constitution, police and public order were entrusted to the states and the task of defence to the Centre. In other words, internal security was the responsibility of the states, supported by the Ministry of Home Affairs, while security against external aggression was the responsibility of the Ministry of Defence. This rather clear allocation of responsibilities was perhaps attributable to the desire of the founding fathers to permit the Centre to focus on the enormous tasks of socio-economic development, laying the foundations of democratic institutions and building a strong and self-reliant India.

It was only after the country had faced external aggressions (1962, 1965, 1971), and encountered an array of serious domestic problems that the preamble to the Constitution was amended to include a provision for 'the Unity and Integrity of the Nation' (Forty-second Amendment, 1976).

While the original Constitution contained elaborate prescriptions regarding the fundamental rights of citizens, there was no clause pertaining to their duties to the nation, not even in respect of the country's security. The provision introduced in 1976 stipulated that while citizens shall enjoy their fundamental rights of liberty of expression, faith and worship, and equality of opportunity, they shall also have the fundamental duty to protect the unity and the integrity of the nation, to defend the country, to volunteer for national service, etc. However, to this day, no legal framework has been provided for the enforcement of these duties, nor to prevent their infringement. The provision has thus remained inoperative.

The Forty-second Amendment also provided that while citizens would continue to enjoy their freedoms of 'speech and expression', 'to assemble peaceably and without arms' and 'to form associations or unions', reasonable restrictions could be imposed in the interest of upholding the integrity and sovereignty of India, and of ensuring the security of India. In other words, notwithstanding the vast array of judicial pronouncements on the Fundamental Rights, the essential objective of the amendment was to provide safeguards against the unbridled enjoyment of these rights which may lead to disturbance of public order or prejudice the unity and integrity of India.

The Constitution authorizes the legislature to frame laws for preventive detentions for reasons connected with the security of the state. Also, it provides that when the president proclaims an Emergency, fundamental rights would remain suspended, and the legislature would be competent to make any law it deems appropriate. The executive, at the same time, shall be at liberty to take any action, even if it contravenes or restricts the rights guaranteed by the Constitution.

The Constitution also stipulated that it shall be the duty of the Union to protect every state against external aggression and internal disturbances, and to ensure that the government of every state is carried on in accordance with the provisions of the Constitution. In the event of failure of any state to ensure constitutional governance, the president can hold that a situation has arisen in which the government of the state concerned cannot be carried on in accordance with the provisions of the Constitution. Thus, in the event of a political breakdown in any state, or in the event of the failure of the state to comply with the federal directives which might affect national solidarity, the Union can exercise its coercive power to maintain the democratic form of government and impose president's rule. Although B.R. Ambedkar had argued in the Constituent Assembly that this provision would remain a 'dead letter', this power has been used over 100 times since 1950!

If the president is satisfied that a grave emergency exists whereby security is threatened by war or external aggression or armed rebellion, an Emergency can be proclaimed in the whole or any part of the country. In the original provision in the Constitution, Emergency could be imposed in the event of a grave situation arising from 'internal disturbance' whereas in the Forty-fourth Amendment (1978) this ground was substituted by 'armed rebellion'. The power to enforce Emergency has been exercised twice on grounds of 'external aggression', in October 1962 after the Chinese intrusion into North-East Frontier Agency (NEFA) and in December 1971 when Pakistan launched an undeclared war on India, and once on the grounds of 'internal disturbance' in June 1975.

EXTERNAL SUPPORT FOR INTERNAL DISTURBANCES

It would be worthwhile to consider whether the provisions in the original Constitution, and the various prescriptions introduced subsequently, have enabled the states and the Centre to adequately maintain internal security. For well over a decade, from the early 1980s, the frontier state of Punjab witnessed a serious breakdown of law and order, resulting in the killing of thousands of persons including a very large number of security personnel and their families. Public functioning and normal life were paralysed, and there were untold losses to the economy of the state, which in turn affected the rest of the country. The trouble in Punjab arose from a demand for the creation of an independent Sikh state. Organized support and encouragement to the secessionist elements was provided by our hostile neighbours who organized training camps for the Sikh youth, and supplied them with propaganda material, funds and lethal arms and ammunition. These covert operations meant that our neighbour was running a proxy war against India, which destabilized the state for almost a decade.

Encouraged by their success in Punjab, our neighbour then organized the induction of trained militants into the Kashmir Valley from around end-1989 and succeeded in creating a situation which led to the dismissal of the elected government. Those inducted into the Valley and later, elsewhere in Jammu and Kashmir (J&K), included not only Kashmiri Muslim youth trained across the border but also hardened Islamic fundamentalist groups in Pakistan and battle-hardened veterans from Afghanistan, West Asia and Africa. This resulted in the unleashing of a wave of terrorism and ethnic cleansing in the Valley, rendering several hundred thousand Kashmiri Hindus homeless and bringing the economy to a dead halt. Though an elected government was restored in late 1996, the terrorist elements are still active.

The situation in several states in the Northeast continues to remain seriously disturbed, especially in Assam, Manipur and Nagaland. In this region too, several of the militant groups continue to receive strong support from across our borders. Incidents of sabotage, subversion and terrorism continue to take place, causing heavy human losses. The uncertain security environment in this region has adversely affected socio-economic development.

Similarly, the extreme left-wing Naxalite group continues to be active in Telangana, Andhra Pradesh and adjoining areas. Bihar had been affected by the criminal activities of factional groups and armed militia whose writ overrode that of the state law enforcement agencies. Public order remains periodically disturbed in several other parts of the country too.

It is important to note that situations seriously affecting the maintenance of internal security have arisen in the past when demands for larger autonomy, or other grievances of minority or ethnic groups have not received sensitive and timely political attention. In Punjab and J&K, the internal situation, aided and abetted from across the border, was quickly transformed into full-blown terrorism.

Besides these specific problems, the overall security environment of the country has also been seriously disturbed by hostile external agencies targeting important political personalities or organizing sabotage to create chaos. In 1984, in the wake of Operation Blue Star in Punjab, Prime Minister Indira Gandhi was assassinated by her own security personnel at her residence. In 1985, Harchand Singh Longowal, the architect of the Punjab Accord, was assassinated in broad daylight while praying in a gurdwara, even though he was heavily protected by the Punjab Police. In 1991, former prime minister Rajiv Gandhi was assassinated by a human bomb. In early 1993, the peace of the metropolitan city of Bombay was shattered by a series of bomb blasts which disrupted normalcy and led to rioting and large-scale communal violence. Besides several thousand killed or injured, economic losses ran into billions, and hitherto unknown tensions and suspicions between Hindus and Muslims in the traditionally secular city of Bombay showed their ugly face. In 1995, Beant Singh, chief minister of Punjab, who was very heavily protected by state and Central police forces, was assassinated on the steps of the state secretariat.

Whatever else may have been the fallout of these incidents, one very specific consequence was that they have led to the progressive enhancement of protection of important political personalities and public servants in high positions. Today, for instance, if the prime minister has to travel even from his residence to parliament, the route is cleared of all traffic, creating hold-ups and generating public resentment.

STATES AND INTERNAL SECURITY

Since the essential responsibility for the maintenance of law and order rests with the states, it would be useful to review whether they are equipped to adequately discharge this vital obligation. When the founding fathers of our Constitution decided to vest this task in the states, maintenance of law and order was a limited function. Largely, it involved keeping criminal offences under control and making preventive arrests, imposing curfew, or resorting to lathi charge to disperse agitating crowds. If this did not work, tear gas was used and, in the event of a crowd turning violent, the state armed police, under directions of a magistrate, was authorized to fire in the air. And if this too did not work, orders were given to fire at the advancing mob to incapacitate the front ranks but not to kill. But things have changed. We are now faced with highly motivated and trained terrorist groups which deploy state-of-the-art weaponry, including remote-controlled gadgets of destruction. The state police forces do not possess the required capability and resources to deal with the proxy war that obtains in J&K and the states of the north-east region. While the home ministry has been providing technical guidance, training and financial support to upgrade and modernize the state police, the sad reality is that barring one or two states, almost all the constabularies and the officer cadres of most states have been politicized and communalized. There is continuous political and extralegal interference in the functioning of the police, which has led to the destruction of the command-and-control structures.

Further, political interference in recruitment has compromised the prescribed educational and physical fitness standards of those enlisted. The training, appointment and promotion of personnel have also been adversely affected. Even the higher appointments, including those of state DGPs (directors general of police), are invariably influenced by considerations of caste, community and politics, without heed to seniority, competence, professionalism or proven integrity. The appointment of pliable commanding officers has resulted in the loss of morale, indiscipline and unreliability of forces in times of crises.

In the past several years, public complaints by social activist groups and the National Human Rights Commission (NHRC) have resulted in the trial of a growing number of police personnel for serious acts of omission and commission. Serving senior officers and even DGPs have been taken into custody and charged with serious offences. Police personnel of all ranks are presently serving jail sentences.

Over the years, the powers of the home ministry have been progressively diluted. All that it retains is a highly fractured control over the management of the Indian Police Service (IPS). The charge of the ministry is often entrusted to ministers with inadequate experience and standing in the Cabinet and the appointment of home secretaries with indifferent credentials have resulted in diluting the home ministry's internal capability and its influence over the states. The states have also progressively displayed a declining concern about the effective management of internal security.

The requirements of the police and intelligence organizations have not been regularly assessed and provided for in the annual budgets. Consequently, over the years, the strength of the armed police forces in most of the states has not been adequately enlarged to meet changing requirements. Worse, even the forces which are actually available are not adequately trained, equipped or led in order to effectively meet emerging security situations. The broad pattern that we see today, all over the country, is the pressing demand on the home ministry by the states to provide the required assistance to deal with deteriorating law and order situations.

Having failed to compel the states to be self-reliant in discharging their constitutional obligation, the Centre has had no choice but to gradually increase the strength of the Central paramilitary forces (CPMF) and yield to the unending demands for the deployment of these forces. Since the early 1980s, under pressure from the states, the home ministry has been deploying elements of CPMF for internal security management. This continued over-deployment is an infringement of the CPMF's statutory roles.

Among the CPMF, the Central Reserve Police Force (CRPF) has the mandate for providing assistance to the states for internal security management. The Assam Rifles (AR) has similar obligations, traditionally confined to the north-eastern region. Both these CPMF are of pre-1947 vintage. Several new units were created after 1950. The Indo-Tibetan Border Police (ITBP) was specially raised after the 1962 war with China to guard the mountainous and high-altitude borders. In the aftermath of the 1965 Indo-Pak war, the Border Security Force (BSF) was established to guard the north-west frontier, and the Central Industrial Security Force (CISF), created later, was given the task of providing security to public sector undertakings.

However, since problems first arose in Punjab and later in J&K and the North-east, the home ministry has been compelled to deploy elements of any available CPMF for internal security duties, even at the cost of thinning their presence at the frontiers assigned to them. Thus, very large elements of the BSF have remained deployed in J&K and the Northeast. Likewise, significant elements of the ITBP were withdrawn from the mountainous borders to perform internal security roles in the plains. Considering the overall security situation in the country, even the Election Commission of India asks for large-scale deployment of CPMF to ensure free and fair polls in the states and during parliamentary elections. Such uninterrupted large-scale deployment of CPMF all over the country has resulted in compromising their training standards and consequently affected their morale and discipline.

To deal with the serious situations in Punjab, J&K and the Northeast, the Centre has been compelled to also involve the army. Such deployments of the armed forces have jeopardized their training programmes and their preparedness for guarding the frontiers. Due to its prolonged involvements in J&K and the Northeast, the army, furthermore, has had to face allegations of infringement of human rights, torture, custodial death and the like. This exposure has tarnished the image of the army, leading to understandable resentment among its ranks.

Ever since the emergence of terrorism, the concerned states and the Centre have had a tendency to attribute them entirely to the proxy war waged by the 'foreign hand'. By all accounts, the Centre has hardly done anything more than 'rushing' contingents of the CPMF or deploying the army in affected areas. There is no evidence of the 'foreign hand' having been objectively analysed and a well-considered plan launched to counter it as required. There is also no evidence to suggest that the Central intelligence agencies have been able to identify the elements of domestic support which have enabled the adversary agencies to operate freely for so many years and extend their networks in various parts of our country.

Having succeeded in destabilizing Punjab and J&K for several years and having gained headway in the Northeast, the external agencies happily proceeded to infiltrate across the seas and land several tonnes of high explosives on the west coast of Maharashtra. This delivery enabled their agents to execute the series of bomb blasts which shook Bombay in March 1993, causing communal violence and large-scale human and economic loss. Air-space has also been used for subversive intrusion. That our skies too were not inviolate was demonstrated beyond doubt when in late 1995 a foreign aircraft, flying from Karachi to ostensible destinations in South-east Asia, air-dropped lethal munitions in Purulia (see Appendix 2), in north Bengal.

Then again, our extensive border with Nepal is virtually open with only a few check-posts at fixed points. In recent years, our hostile neighbour has established networks along the Indo-Nepal border as well as Kathmandu and other parts of Nepal to propagate religious fundamentalism and carry out subversive missions in India. Hostile agencies have been operating in our north-eastern region from various vantage points across the Indo-Bangladesh border. The same is the case with the Indo-Myanmar border, some stretches of which are covered with forest and are therefore inaccessible. Insurgent and subversive groups – active in Manipur and Nagaland for years – have their links and support bases in Myanmar. The flow of illegal immigrants from Bangladesh has resulted in serious demographic imbalances in the Northeast and has generated a situation which seriously affects the security of several states in this region.

Another threat to national security is the fact that India has emerged as perhaps the busiest transit route for the movement of narcotics and illicit drugs from the countries of the golden triangle in the Northeast and those of the golden crescent in the Northwest. The multi-trillion-dollar drug trade also finances the sale of illegal arms and the most sophisticated weapons of destruction which have proliferated in the subcontinent. The unlimited resources of the narco-terrorist networks, some of which are backed by fundamentalist groups, have the potential of causing untold damage to the country.

In addition, the states have failed in establishing efficient intelligence organizations that are vital to security management. They rely almost entirely on the inputs provided by the Centre which has two agencies: the Intelligence Bureau (IB) and Research and Analysis Wing (RAW).

EXTERNALLY INSPIRED SUBVERSIVE NETWORKS

Considering the situations in J&K and the Northeast and the investigation reports of the Central Bureau of Investigation (CBI), it is evident that powers inimical to our interests have created subversive networks in the sensitive and vulnerable parts of our country. Supplies of the most sophisticated explosives, remote-control devices and other means of sabotage and destruction continue to find their way into various parts of India. The investigations of the CBI in the Bombay bomb blasts of 1993 and in several other major cases of sabotage have all pointed to the existence of networks with strong cross-border support and linkages.

From 1980 onwards it has been progressively established that besides the proxy war waged by our neighbour, which has had the most serious ramifications in Punjab, J&K and the Northeast, the security of India is increasingly being threatened by the operation of criminal and mafia elements which indulge in organized crime, money laundering and smuggling. The scale of such activities, revealed in recently exposed scams and scandals, shows that the functioning of political parties and decision-making authorities is being systematically subverted.

The existence of a nexus between politicians, bureaucrats and crime syndicates was reported in a study undertaken by the home ministry in mid-1993, after the bomb blasts in Bombay. If the home ministry was alive to its responsibilities, this report (see Appendix 1) should have acted as a catalyst to the designing of an integrated action plan, involving all concerned state and Central agencies, so as to effectively counter the most serious threats posed to our national security. The unending exposures of money-laundering and corruption at the highest places have also pointed to politicians who have been paid large sums of 'black money' in exchange for favours and immunity from the law. Such widespread corruption – subverting the functioning of vital government agencies – has frightening implications for national security. It poses a serious threat to the very unity and integrity of India.

It is clear that the existing Central intelligence apparatus is grossly inadequate. Besides failures on various fronts, the Central ministries and agencies concerned with the management of national security have not been able to work in close coordination. The parliamentary committee which investigated the airdropping of lethal munitions in Purulia by a foreign aircraft revealed that even though the IB had received advance information about the possibility of such an occurrence and had passed it on to the home ministry, the latter failed to realize its import and did not transmit it promptly to all concerned.

The IB has still to be provided a charter of duties and responsibilities, including the manner in which its work should interface with RAW. The Joint Intelligence Committee (JIC) – set up as the apex agency to collect, collate and analyse intelligence inputs from all appropriate agencies and draw up threat assessments – has become virtually defunct. The various concerned agencies are reluctant to share available intelligence with the JIC, and little attention is paid to whatever reports and analyses the latter is able to generate. Today, we have a situation where no single authority can be held accountable for major security lapses.

With the deregulation of industry under the New Economic Policy (1991) and the opening up of India's markets, there is growing movement in and out of the country by foreign companies, corporations and agencies, all of which are apparently interested only in extending their industrial and business interests in India. With the highly porous security systems that we have, there are no means of timely and adequate monitoring of these new flows, especially the large-scale monetary transactions inherent in an open market economy. Bank and stock market scams show that effective surveillance mechanisms have still to be established. The nascent euphoria of our economic system, attracting large-scale foreign investments and yielding higher rates of growth, must not distract us from the importance of ensuring our national security interests.

Experience elsewhere in the world has shown how certain foreign powers have carried out covert operations to subvert the national interest of targeted countries and manipulated them to extend their own economic, political and security interests. As demonstrated by several African and Latin American countries, this was done by corrupting the political leadership and the top echelons of the bureaucracies and even the armed forces. In our immediate neighbourhood, Afghanistan has been destroyed in the crossfire of competing interests. Now overtaken by extreme fundamentalist forces, the conflagration in the country has generated bands of trained terrorists, most of whom are sponsored by our neighbour and have been operating in J&K. One of these groups destroyed the historical Charar-i-Sharief shrine in Kashmir in 1995, intending to create an upheaval which would further postpone the election process in J&K which was then under way.

Covert operations in several parts of India, organized from across the borders, have kept the state governments concerned and the Centre fully engaged in restoring normalcy and undoing the subversion of governance structures. Besides the tens of thousands killed, the destabilizing of these areas has resulted in enormous economic losses and serious retardation of the developmental processes. The infusion of external factors in internal security management has led to a situation in which it is no longer possible to view internal and external security issues separately. These have become inextricably intermeshed and cannot be disentangled by executive fiat or populist political statements.

Nor are the old concepts of law and order maintenance valid any longer. With sustained covert operations organized by our adversaries, including the emergence of subversive networks fomenting fundamentalism, supporting organized sabotage, militancy and terrorism, internal security management today poses an extremely complex and difficult challenge. However, the Ministry of Defence can no longer concern itself only with external security. The defence forces cannot merely look outwards and watch the frontiers when the rear has been subverted and destabilized. Nor can the home ministry take the position that, constitutionally, it can concern itself only with those aspects of internal security management which the states are unable to tackle. The highly motivated and trained networks which operate in our country are not constrained by state or national boundaries.

The time has come to view all internal and external security issues together and design countermeasures which take into account activities on all fronts, irrespective of whether they fall within the purview of the states or various ministries and organizations at the Centre. Such a crucial task cannot be handled by the home ministry. In its present form this ministry can at best seek some degree of coordination among the numerous Central departments and agencies concerned with the maintenance of internal security. As the Purulia incident demonstrated, the home ministry cannot be relied upon even for effective coordination.

India has a very large and growing population, half of which is illiterate and one-third of which lives below the poverty line. Political parties at all levels have been exploiting the illiterate, backward and vulnerable segments of our society for short-term electoral gains. A national policy of reservations and various other measures have been implemented to enable empowerment of the people. While it is far too early to assess the ultimate benefit of such moves, it can hardly be suggested that the existing interplay of political forces in the states and the Centre is leading us towards greater stability and social cohesion. On the contrary, the commitments of our polity to secure and hold power at any cost has led to growing communalism and religious revivalism, generating nationwide distrust and antagonism among various segments of our society.

Today, India is surcharged with latent tensions which can be readily exploited to spark off confrontations, conflicts and violence. Such a scenario provides an excellent playground for adverse external powers and their agencies to sabotage, subvert and destabilize the governance of our country. National security can no longer be safeguarded by seeking refuge in the existing constitutional arrangements and division of responsibilities between the Centre and the states. Nor can these grave and complex problems be tackled by the home ministry alone, as its capability and resourcefulness have been progressively diluted over the years.

Myriad streams flow into the river of national security. The ingredients of each such flow have to be monitored by professionally trained and dedicated personnel who operate within well-designed structures, each of which is functionally linked so that the entire superstructure is fully accountable and answerable. The various ministries – home, defence, foreign affairs, industry, commerce, science and technology, and finance – as well as the large number of other agencies concerned with the management of national security, have to put their heads together and be fully involved in evolving an effective security management structure. The elements against which the country is pitted, and whose activities need to be pre-empted and neutralized, are supported by enormous resources with the capability to corrupt, sabotage and subvert our national interest at a time of their choosing. We live in a world of speedy movement, high technology and rapid information. Our security systems and structures have to be correspondingly competent and combative. No time can be lost in leisurely academic debates about what is required to be done.

If the unity, integrity and sovereignty of the country have to be safeguarded, the necessary structures and systems must be established within a time frame and they must be held fully accountable for ensuring the security of our nation on all fronts.

2

Challenges Facing Internal Security Management*

In any discussion on national security, it would be useful to keep in mind the physical parameters of our concerns. India is the seventh largest country in the world. We have land frontiers with six countries and maritime borders with five countries. Our borders with Pakistan and China are militarized; those with Pakistan generate a variety of threats to our country.

We must also remember that our country represents an immense cultural and geographical diversity and socio-religious traditions which go back to 5,000 years of recorded history. The people of India comprise multiracial, multi-religious, multilingual and multicultural societies. Every major religion in the world is practised in India; the Muslim population here is the second largest in the world, significantly larger than that of Pakistan. The roots of India's secular and pluralistic traditions are embedded deep in our history.

India's internal security problems, arising from varied sources, are influenced by a host of factors, among which are its past history, geography, colonial legacy, a burgeoning population, economic disparities and complex socio-cultural and ethno-religious traditions which interplay freely in our secular democracy. As developments

---

* First published in *India International Quarterly*, New Delhi: India International Centre, 1996.

in the past have shown, regional and global developments impact significantly on our security interests.

India is a Union of states. Our Constitution demarcates the executive and legislative powers of the Union and the states. It would be useful to recall the Sarkaria Commission's view that the states should themselves handle problems of law and order and the Centre should provide aid to a state only when a specific request to that effect is received. In such situations, the Centre may deploy one or more of its police forces and/or the army in aid of the civil authority (Item 2A, List I, Seventh Schedule).

Several years ago the Ministry of Home Affairs had reported, in its forty-third report to the standing committee of parliament, that about 40 per cent of the districts in the country are affected by grave public disorders of militancy, insurgency and ethnic strife. Against this background, it may not be worthwhile to draw up a chronological list of the serious internal security problems faced by the country in the past. However, it would be relevant to recognize that while it is the constitutional responsibility of the states to maintain peace and public order, the ground realities have changed most significantly in the past few years. Unlike in the initial period after Independence, the state police forces have, for well over two decades now, been called upon to deal with serious disturbances created by highly trained and motivated insurgent and terrorist groups which possess unlimited resources, sophisticated weaponry and communication systems. This should be kept in mind while undertaking any assessment of the manner in which the states have been discharging their constitutional responsibility to maintain law and order. The fact is, almost all the states have defaulted in their crucial obligation to progressively expand and maintain fully trained and equipped police forces, in adequate strength, to meet the rising challenges to the maintenance of internal security.

It would not be out of place here to briefly refer to some of the gross failures which are shared by almost all the states and have a continuing adverse impact on internal security management. Despite the passage of five decades since we gained Independence, the state police organizations continue to function under a colonial statute, the Police Act of 1861. Enacted by our imperial masters nearly a century and a half ago, this legislation is altogether incompatible with the requirements of policing within a democratic framework. This serious constraint is compounded by the continued neglect and, worse still, the systematic erosion of discipline and professionalism, which is the result of sustained politicization of the state police forces and interference in their day-to-day functioning. While the states would need to take various necessary measures to improve their administrative apparatus for security without any further delay, the most urgent requirement is to depoliticize the functioning of the police departments and, side by side, allocate the required resources to ensure the maintenance of adequately trained and equipped forces, in the required strength, in every state.

Ever since Pakistan's initial adventure in fomenting militancy in Punjab, the Centre has, for obvious reasons been engaged in tackling emerging disorders by deploying the armed forces of the Union, i.e., the Central police forces and, as required, the army and other defence forces, in the affected areas. Of course, the restoration of normalcy in any disturbed area inevitably involves the application of the state's coercive power, which means deploying the required quantum of Central forces to bring the disturbed area under control.

Faced with problems on various fronts and the unending demands from the state governments for the deployment of Central forces, even in situations which could have been handled by the states, the Ministry of Home Affairs is perpetually engaged in mobilizing and making available the required assistance even if this involves pulling away the forces guarding the border.

This also means that the Centre has not had the opportunity, or the time and adequate administrative and other required resources, to devote due attention to the factors which have contributed to the emergence of internal disorders in various parts of the country.

Going by past experience of combating insurgencies, especially in the Northeast, it would be unwise to assume that the ultimate resolution of serious breakdowns of public order relate merely to the speed and efficiency with which the state police or the Central armed forces carry out operations. Indeed, contrary to the mistaken belief in certain quarters, the ultimate responsibility of dealing with an internal security problem cannot be 'handed over' to any of the armed forces of the Union, under any circumstances. Nor can state governments abdicate the constitutional responsibility to run the administration.

The truth is that prolonged deployment of Central police forces or the army to carry out counter-insurgency operations cannot restore normalcy unless the chief ministers, their cabinets and the entire administrative apparatus, which functions under their control, devote prompt and simultaneous attention to providing effective governance. They also need to pay heed to resolving the day-to-day difficulties faced by common people on account of the disruption of normal functioning caused by an insurgent situation. It is, therefore, of vital importance that the chief ministers and the government machinery which runs under their direction devote special attention to ensure the time-bound implementation of all schemes and programmes which promote the welfare of the people at large, especially those who have been seriously affected and disadvantaged by the disorder being tackled by the security forces.

In the past, state-level bodies, called by various names, have been set up to coordinate counter-insurgency operations by the security forces. It is necessary that the functioning of such apex bodies is supervised by the chief ministers to ensure that normal administration is not suspended merely because the security forces are engaged in carrying out operations in the state. If normalcy is to be restored, the security forces and the civil administration must discharge their respective roles in unison under the overall direction of the state chief minister.

The states must be sensitive in understanding and critically assessing the likely consequences of an emerging situation and, based on a careful analysis, promptly implement the required remedial measures. This would, inter alia, require the political leadership of the states and the concerned senior functionaries to interact in a timely and meaningful way with the leaders or representatives of the agitating segment of society.

Experience has shown that lack of timely concern, or failure to deal understandingly with the demands of the aggrieved elements, invariably leads to enhanced estrangements possibly leading to violence. When such situations get out of hand, the traditional approach is to deal with them merely as law and order problems. In many such cases the disgruntled elements, abetted and supported by hostile external agencies, are easily persuaded to adopt the gun culture. And when such developments take place, we see the beginnings of militancy and insurgency. So it is necessary to ensure that the coercive powers of the state are applied only after due deliberation. While dealing effectively with an emerging disorder, the states must remain equally responsible for taking timely measures to identify and deal with the root causes of any situation which is likely to escalate into an internal security problem. This calls for timely and systematic attention to the socio-economic problems of the masses and also due concern for their political demands and aspirations.

The despair and consequent alienation of the disadvantaged communities is usually heightened by the social and economic exploitation to which they are subjected. Feudal systems are still in existence in several parts of the country where much-needed land, agrarian and other reforms have still to be implemented. It is most unfortunate that besides the economic disparities and severe disadvantages from which they suffer, the neglected segments of society are also subjected to continued harassments, which arises from the exploitation of religious, ethnic and caste factors by various political parties for electoral gains.

Besides the failure to pursue the avowed goals of a welfare

state and deliver social and economic justice to the masses, the states have also failed to respond to the felt needs and aspirations of ethnic and tribal groups and communities, most of whom live in remote, difficult and underdeveloped areas. It has been seen that the demands of such neglected communities are ignored for prolonged periods and considered essentially in terms of the likely electoral gains to the parties in power. Such an attitude has contributed to these communities losing faith and trust in their elected representatives and the state governments.

Another factor which causes despair and anger among the underprivileged is the failure of the states to efficiently execute poverty alleviation schemes and programmes. The large financial outlays and outright grants provided to the states by the Centre for such programmes are not properly utilized. These are often illegitimately diverted to ease the ways-and-means position of the state exchequers and, in many cases, the money is embezzled. Needless to say, such gross failures result in creating hopelessness, cynicism and consequential alienation among the poorest segments of society.

Such failures are due to maladministration, unaccountability and corruption. Notwithstanding the endless public criticism over the past many years, effective steps have still to be taken to deal with corruption at the highest levels and enforce efficiency, honesty and accountability in the functioning of the public services. The Lokpal Bill has been awaiting enactment for nearly four decades and the functioning of the Lokayukts, established in many states, has still to bring the dishonest to book. Corruption weakens the very foundations of the administrative and legal framework and disrupts the rule of law. Hence, eradicating corruption from the functioning of the government apparatus is a sine qua non of internal security.

The lack of accountability which has permeated government functioning has, among other things, contributed to the growth of threatening linkages between unprincipled politicians, dishonest public servants and the criminal and mafia elements. Following the serial bomb blasts in Bombay in March 1993, which were carried out by the Dawood Ibrahim gang in concert with the ISI, a committee appointed by the Centre under the chairmanship of the then Union home secretary, had submitted its report (see Appendix 1) in September 1993, which concluded that crime syndicates and mafia organizations had established themselves in various parts of the country and developed significant muscle and money power to carry out their activities with impunity. It was brought out that such syndicates thrived on the strength of their linkages with political leaders, governmental functionaries and other influential elements. The action taken on this criminal nexus report has not been made public.

While there are various factors which contribute to the lack of good governance in the states, one major reason is that political parties in power remain perennially preoccupied with retaining their position, by whatever means, instead of being engaged in promoting the welfare of their people. This unfortunate situation is further vitiated by rampant corruption and lack of accountability in public services at all levels of functioning. Efforts to contain and reduce corruption do not yield the desired outcome as the tainted elements in the administrative system enjoy the patronage and protection of their political masters who have placed them in key positions. An extremely worrying aspect of this situation is that functionaries of highly questionable integrity, who maintain close linkages with criminal and anti-national elements, continue to hold responsible positions in the administrative apparatus. The potential of such elements subverting the functioning of government from within poses a serious threat to the security of the state.

Problems arising from the failure of governance have been compounded by the continuing, determined efforts of hostile foreign agencies to destabilize the country by investing enormous resources for spreading religious fundamentalism, generating conflicts and perpetrating violence and subversion. The result is that, today, we face an extremely worrying situation in which our internal security concerns have got inextricably interwoven with the management of external security.

A stable security environment cannot be engendered merely by promulgating new laws. In the final analysis, every citizen must discharge his duty to uphold and protect the sovereignty, unity and integrity of the country. It is unfortunate that while the vast majority of our people are concerned about their fundamental rights, there are not very many, even among the educated classes, who are even aware of their fundamental duties, laid down in Article 51A of the Constitution. Even if action were to be taken to enforce the fundamental duties of our citizens, which, most regrettably, has not so far been done, it would be unsound to assume that the citizenry of India would overnight become imbued with patriotic feelings and would work to protect national interests if the environment continues to be vitiated by discrimination, corruption and injustice. The requisite environment can be engendered only if the states demonstrate and ensure that the laws of the land apply equally to all, including the rich and influential and the highest placed public servants. Side by side, it must be ensured that no injustice is done to the poor and disadvantaged segments of society as this would result only in promoting distrust and despair among the masses, further eroding their loyalties.

But lawlessness cannot be controlled and internal security maintained unless the entire framework of the criminal justice system functions with speed, fairness and transparent honesty. From the statistics collected and annually published by the Ministry of Home Affairs it may be observed that while, on an average, over five million criminal cases are registered every year, well over twenty million cases continue to await trial in court, and the number of pending cases is progressively increasing. Besides the enormous logistical inadequacies in the justice delivery system, the integrity of the magistracy and the subordinate judiciary is seriously tainted. In the recent past, serious allegations of financial and moral corruption have been raised even against judges of the high courts. Needless to say, the most urgent measures need to be taken to clean up the justice administration apparatus and enlarge and strengthen it to ensure speedy trials.

Another cause for serious concern is that while we continue to have hundreds of altogether obsolete and irrelevant laws, most of which were enacted during the colonial period, we do not have an adequately stringent law, applicable all over the country, which can meet the requirements of effectively dealing with terrorist offences, cybercrimes and the fast growing areas of organized criminality, which pose a grave threat to the nation's unity and integrity. We also do not have a federal crime agency which can deal with the serious offences committed by criminal networks whose activities spread across several states or even the entire country. We also need a comprehensive law for dealing with serious economic offences which, if not checked in time, have the potential of disrupting the national economy.

Today, terrorist and criminal networks operate in a borderless world and, needless to say, the grave challenges posed by their activities cannot be tackled if the various law enforcing agencies continue to operate within their respective limited jurisdictions. What is urgently required is an appropriate legal framework and a well-planned strategy which must be executed in effective coordination between the Centre and the states.

Many of the fundamental factors which generate grievances among the people, some of which may cause serious internal disorders, would start getting resolved when they are empowered and communities are enabled to manage most of their affairs. Such a goal was sought to be achieved through the crucial seventy-third and seventy-fourth amendments to the Constitution. The states would need to pursue this objective with greater commitment and at a faster pace than has been seen in the past few decades.

The Centre on its part must continue with its ongoing efforts to allocate progressively increasing resources to the Ministry of

Home Affairs for better internal security management and taking all necessary measures to effectively enforce a constant vigil in all parts of the country. Side by side, the states, which are receiving significant assistance from the Centre to improve their security apparatus, would have to improve their functioning without any further loss of time. Among the most urgent steps required to be taken by the states is the depoliticization of the functioning of the police organizations and the strengthening of their intelligence wings which should operate in close and effective collaboration with the Central intelligence agencies.

Most importantly, a holistic view needs to taken of all our security concerns and a comprehensive strategy should be planned and executed in coordination by the Centre and the states, to effectively safeguard national security.

To conclude, there cannot be any rule of law except the constitutional rule of law. The command of the Constitution must be scrupulously obeyed by the executive, legislature and the judiciary. Any threat to constitutional values poses a threat to the very foundations of the polity and society and, by consequence to national security.

3

Need for Effective Security Management[*]

There is an urgent need today for the Central government to secure appropriate understandings with the states for finalizing a national security policy and putting in place a modern, fully coordinated security management system which can effectively negate any emerging challenge to the territorial security, unity and integrity of India. It would be useful, at the very outset, to state that the term 'national security' could be defined to comprise external security, which relates to safeguarding the country against war and external aggression, and internal security which relates to the maintenance of public order and normalcy within the country.

The first generation of India's security analysts, who focused attention almost entirely on issues relating to external security, had found it convenient to distinguish issues relating to external and internal security. However, such a segregated approach is no longer feasible, particularly after the advent of terrorism, which has introduced extremely frightening dimensions to the internal security environment. I would go further to say that issues of internal and external security management have been inextricably intertwined ever since Pakistan launched a proxy war in J&K in

* First Air Commodore Jasjit Singh Memorial Lecture organized by Centre for Air Power Studies, New Delhi; delivered on 18 July 2014.

early 1990 and Pakistan-based jihadi terrorists started establishing networks across our country.

It is also extremely important that, besides all necessary steps being taken for safeguarding India's territorial security and establishing a very strong machinery to counter terrorism, close attention is also paid for effectively securing other important arenas, particularly those relating to food, water, environment and ecology, science and technology, energy, nuclear power, economy, cyber security, et al.

The more serious problems in recent years have emanated from Pakistan's continuing proxy war in J&K; jihadi terrorism, which has been progressively spreading its reach; and the destructive activities that the left-wing extremist groups have been carrying out for decades now. Apart from these, the serious unrest created by the still active insurgencies in the north-eastern region and incidents of serious communal violence, which have been erupting in the various states from time to time, have to be taken into account.

Mention must also be made of the steadily growing activities of the Indian Mujahidin (IM), a terror group which has its roots in Pakistan. Another phenomenon, relatively more recent, relates to the emergence of certain radical counter-groups which have been organized with the primary objective of countering the jihadi terror networks. The activities of such counter-groups have the potential of spreading disharmony and divisiveness, which could generate widespread communal violence and result in irreparably damaging the secular fabric of our democracy.

India's hinterland continues to remain the prime focus of Pakistan-based terror groups, particularly the Lashkar-e-Taiba (LeT) and IM. In the recent past, indigenous groups comprising elements of the Students' Islamic Movement of India (SIMI) and Al-Ummah have perpetrated serious violence in the country and, notwithstanding its frequent denials, Pakistan remains steadfastly committed to harbouring anti-India terror groups on its soil.

The activities of the left-wing extremist groups, which have been continuing their armed struggle for the past several decades to capture political power, pose an extremely serious internal security challenge. While there may have been a marginal decline in the scale of incidents and the number of killings in the past few years, there has been a marked increase in the gruesome attacks by Naxalite groups on the security forces.

NATIONAL SECURITY POLICY

Having referred to some of the more worrying concerns on the homeland front, it would be useful to examine whether we have established the required institutions which are capable of effectively meeting the emerging threats. As per the provisions in our Constitution, it is the duty of the Union to protect every state against external aggression and internal disturbance.

In the past, the country has had to encounter external aggression on several occasions and no significant issues have arisen about the Union's role and responsibility in this regard. However, not all the states have accepted so far the Central government's authority to enact and enforce federal laws for dealing with terror acts, cyber offences and other major crimes which have all-India ramifications. The states have also been opposing the Central government's authority to establish new security management agencies with pan-India jurisdiction. It has been argued by some state governments that it is the constitutional prerogative of the states to manage law and order within their territories and that the Centre has no basis for interfering in this area.

Undoubtedly, the states are constitutionally mandated to make all required laws in regard to police and public order, take all necessary executive decisions, establish adequate police organizations and manage appropriate security systems for effectively maintaining law and order within their territories. However, looking back over the serious law and order failures which have occurred in various parts of the country in the past several decades, it cannot be said that there have been no failures and that all the states have a sustained record of preventing any breach in the maintenance of peace and security within their jurisdictions.

One of the more significant contributory factors in this context is the states' failure to maintain adequate intelligence organizations and well-trained police forces in the required strength to effectively maintain internal security within their territories. On many occasions the states have also displayed a lack of political will to deal with an emerging situation on their own. Instead, the general practice, which has evolved over the past many years, has been for the affected state to rush to the Union home ministry for the urgent deployment of Central armed police forces for restoring normalcy in the disturbed area.

Another factor which has adversely affected internal security management relates to the progressive erosion of the professionalism of the state police forces. This regrettable decline has taken place because of political interference in the day-to-day functioning of the constabularies. Such interference has, over the years, caused untold damage and most adversely affected the accountability, morale and the very integrity of the state police forces.

In the annual all-India internal security conferences organized by the Union home ministry, many chief ministers have been taking the position that internal security cannot be managed effectively because the states do not have the resources for enlarging and modernizing their police and security related organizations. For over two decades now, the Union home ministry has been providing annual allocations for the modernization of the state police forces. However, it is a matter for serious concern that the Central government has failed to evolve a national security management policy which clearly delineates the roles and responsibilities of the Central and state governments. Nonetheless, whenever called upon to do so, the Central government has been consistently assisting the states by deploying Central police forces, and even the army, for restoring normalcy.

Considering the gravity of the security threats, it is important that the Central government takes the most urgent steps for finalizing the national security policy and the machinery for its administration, in consultations with the states. The national security policy must leave no doubt or uncertainty whatsoever about the Central government's authority for taking all necessary steps for pre-empting or preventing disturbances in any part of the country. Regrettably, the Central government has not always been able to deploy its forces for protecting even its own assets which are located in the various states.

Under Article 256 of the Constitution, the executive power of the Union extends to giving of such directions to a state as may appear to the Government of India to be necessary for that purpose. However, over the years, the Union home ministry's general approach has been to merely issue cautionary notes and not any directives in regard to an emerging situation. This approach, of sending out advisories, has not proved effective and, over the years, varied internal disturbances have taken place in different parts of the country, some of which have caused large human, economic and other losses. The circumstances which led to the demolition of the Babri Masjid, and the grave consequences thereof suffered by the nation, are still far too fresh in our memories to call for any retelling.

After the national security policy has been finalized, the Central government will have to undertake, in collaboration with the states, a countrywide review of the existing security management apparatus and draw up a plan for restructuring and revamping it within a stipulated timeframe. While playing their part in such an exercise, the states would need to accept the important role they are required to play in national security management and demonstrate their unconditional commitment to working closely with each other and the Central government to protect the unity and integrity of the country.

For nearly two decades now, there have been repeated pronouncements that the Central government is promulgating a law for dealing with identified federal offences and establishing a central agency which would have the authority of taking cognizance of, and investigating, crimes which have serious inter-state or nationwide ramifications for national security. The proposal of setting up the National Counter Terrorism Centre (NCTC), for instance, has continued to be debated for the past several years. A number of states, which have been opposed to the establishment of NCTC in its present form, have suggested that the proposed framework of this body should be entirely revised in consultation with the states. Some other states have urged that NCTC should not be established through an executive order but through an Act of parliament and that it should function under the administrative control of the Union home ministry instead of under the Intelligence Bureau.

As acts of terror and other federal offences cannot be dealt with by the existing security management apparatus, it is necessary that the Central government undertakes urgent discussions with the chief ministers to resolve all the doubts and issues raised by the states. Towards this objective, the Union home ministry could beneficially utilize the aegis of the Inter-State Council (ISC), of which the prime minister is the chairperson.

It would also be useful for the Central government to consider various possible initiatives for promoting trust and understanding between New Delhi and the state capitals. To begin with, it could consider inducting representatives of the states in the National Security Advisory Board and the National Security Council, even if this is to be done on a rotational basis. The Centre could also consider setting up an empowered committee of home ministers of states to discuss and arrive at pragmatic solutions to various important security related issues, including the long-pending proposal to set up the National Counter Terrorism Centre (NCTC).

Some of the doubts voiced by the states about the management of security related issues arise from the style of functioning of institutions which are exclusively controlled by the Central government. Perhaps a more productive approach may lie in certain important institutions being jointly run by the Centre and the states. An excellent example in this regard is the Joint Terrorism Task Force (JTTF), established by the United States of America in the aftermath of 9/11. The Joint Terrorism Task Force located in various cities across the US include representatives from the federal, state and municipal enforcement agencies and perform several important roles, including the clearing of all terrorism-related information. Over time, functioning through joint institutions will enable the states to gain a well-informed all-India perspective about the complex and sensitive issues which concern national security management and, in this process, also defuse their perennial complaint about the Central government 'interfering with the powers of the states in the arena of internal security management'.

MODERNIZATION OF STATE POLICE

Needless to stress, if national security is to be satisfactorily managed, the states must effectively maintain internal security within their territories. Towards this end, they must urgently get to work to enlarge and upgrade their intelligence and police organizations and security administration systems. So, it is a matter for serious concern that the annual allocations for police comprise an extremely low percentage of the total budgeted expenditure of all the states and Union territories in the country. The scale of these allocations must be significantly enhanced, particularly keeping in mind that about 80 per cent of the annual state police budgets go towards meeting the salaries and pensions of the constabularies, and virtually no funds remain for undertaking expansion or modernization of the state police forces. Time-bound action would have to be taken to ensure that the sanctioned posts of police personnel, lakhs of which remain vacant for years in the state and Union territory police forces, are filled up on a time-bound basis.

However, the ailments from which the state police forces

have been suffering for decades now will not be cured merely by providing larger budgetary allocations. It is extremely important to ensure that police reforms are carried through without any further delay. It is a matter for utter shame that after nearly seven decades since Independence the police organizations in many states are still functioning under the colonial Police Act of 1861. Most states have also not taken the required steps to implement the Supreme Court's orders regarding the establishment of Police Complaint Authorities and State Security Commissions; segregation of law and order and investigation functions; setting up of separate intelligence and anti-terrorist units and taking varied other actions for establishing modern and accountable police forces which would enable the effective functioning of the security management apparatus.

CRIMINAL JUSTICE SYSTEM

It is also necessary to recognize that national security cannot be safeguarded unless the entire apparatus of the criminal justice system discharges its duties with competence, speed, fairness and complete honesty. In 2013, nearly two crore criminal cases under the Indian Penal Code and special laws were awaiting trial. This sad state of neglect, accompanied by progressively declining conviction rates, has rightly generated the perception that crime is a low-risk and high-profit business in India.

The functioning of the judicial apparatus, particularly at the lower and middle levels, suffers from serious logistical deficiencies – grossly insufficient number of courts and judges, prolonged delays in filling up long-pending vacancies, lack of staff and essential facilities in the courts and so on. Questions are also being repeatedly raised about the competence and integrity of those manning the judicial system. In recent years, allegations of shameful delinquencies have been made even against those who man the highest echelons in the judicial system, up to the august level of the Chief Justice of India!

Therefore, the most urgent measures are required to be implemented for enforcing complete objectivity and fairness in the selection and appointment of judicial officers and judges at all levels. Stringent steps must be taken to enforce the highest judicial standards and accountability to establish a clean and strong judicial system, which restores respect and fear among one and all for the Constitution and the rule of law.

Alongside the cleaning-up and revitalization of the judicial system, it is necessary to weed out all obsolete laws and update and amend other statutes, many of which were enacted during the colonial era or in the early years after Independence, to ensure their continued relevance. For instance, the Indian Evidence Act needs to be urgently reviewed, inter alia, to provide for the permissibility of electronic evidence.

It is also necessary to ensure prompt and professional investigations, competent and time-bound trials, and award of deterrent punishments to all those found guilty of unlawful acts. Towards this end, it is necessary to create cadres of competent investigation officers and criminal law prosecutors and urgently enact a well-considered federal law for dealing with the rapidly increasing economic offences. Drawn up in appropriate consultation with the states, such a comprehensive law should cover the growing spectrum of economic and other major offences, some of which are closely linked with the funding of terror and networks of organized crime.

It would be incorrect to assume that serious threats to national security emanate only from the activities of Naxalites, terror groups and the mafia networks. Corruption at various levels of administration is another factor which adversely impacts our national security interests. Year in and year out, for the past several decades now, major scams and scandals have been getting exposed and India continues to hold a shamefully high position in the global corruption index.

It must be stressed that corruption vitiates and disrupts the rule of law and destroys the very foundations of the administrative and legal apparatus. The prevalence of corrupt practices at various levels generates anger, despair and helplessness among people, compelling them to lose trust in the functioning of the government machinery. Cynicism and the loss of hope engenders an environment which leads to the alienation of the common man, paving the way for attraction to the gun culture and extremist ideologies. Past experience has also shown that corrupt and unseemly elements in the governmental apparatus sabotage national security interests from within, and grave threats are generated when they act in nexus with organized crime and mafia networks.

As regards the subversion of the governmental machinery from within, it would be recalled that the criminal nexus report (see Appendix 1) had cautioned about the emergence of crime syndicates/mafia groups which have built up enormous money and muscle power and are able to carry out their criminal activities with ease and impunity. Hence it becomes even more important to ensure that the national security apparatus functions effectively. And, towards this end, it is imperative that the security management machinery is run by appropriately qualified and especially trained personnel.

NATIONAL INVESTIGATION AGENCY

After the November 2008 terror attack in Mumbai, the government of India had hurriedly enacted a law to set up a National Investigation Agency (NIA), on the pattern of the Federal Bureau of Investigation of USA, to investigate and prosecute terror offenses. As per its legal framework, the NIA has the authority to investigate and prosecute only certain specified offenses which are committed within the country and which affect national security.

The NIA has no extra-territorial jurisdiction and no powers to probe incidents which occur outside India, as for example the recent militant attack on the consulate of India in Herat. The NIA director does not have the powers enjoyed by the directors general of police, to permit an investigating officer dealing with a terror crime to seize or attach property. Also, unlike in the case of the CBI, the NIA is not empowered to depute its investigating officers abroad for direct interactions with a foreign agency that is investigating a major terror act which directly or indirectly affects our national security interests.

The NIA's functioning in the past six years also shows that the police authorities in the states are reluctant and take their own time in handing over to the NIA even major criminal cases which may have serious inter-state or nationwide ramifications. Many offences, including major crimes under the Indian Penal Code (IPC) which may be directly linked to terror activities, have still to be brought under the NIA's jurisdiction. Thus, briefly, the NIA, as presently constituted, does not have the legal authority to take the required action to pre-empt or prevent a terror crime, even when it functions in coordination with the concerned states. The NIA needs to be fully empowered, on the most immediate basis, if it is to serve the purpose for which it was established.

SECURITY MANAGEMENT CONCERNS

Even after the gruesome terror attack in Mumbai in November 2008, our country has still to evolve a national security policy and put in place effective mechanisms for implementing it. Also, the ground has still not been cleared to promulgate a well-considered federal law under which a fully empowered Central agency can take immediate cognizance and promptly proceed to investigate any federal offence, within the country and abroad, without having to lose precious time in seeking varied clearances and going through time-consuming consultative processes. Any delay, which is inherent in working within a consultative system, would virtually ensure the failure of investigations, particularly as the terror groups strike their targets and get away with lightning speed.

In conclusion, then:

i)   India is facing progressively increasing security threats from across its frontiers as well as from within.

ii) The absence of a bipartisan approach has led to several states questioning the Central government's leadership role in national security management. Insofar as the discharge of their own constitutional responsibilities is concerned, most states cannot claim a sustained record of maintaining peace and tranquillity within their own territories.

iii) As a general practice, instead of progressively improving the capability of their police and security maintenance apparatus for effectively dealing with arising disturbances, the states have been perennially seeking assistance from the Union home ministry, whenever a problem is arising in their territories.

iv) While the Central government has been, without any exception, providing assistance to the states by deploying Central police forces, and even the army, for restoring normalcy in the disturbed areas, the states have never been questioned about the reasons for their failure to maintain internal security, nor about their failures to deal with the root causes of the recurring disturbances in their territories.

v)   The Constitution of India prescribes that the states shall be responsible for the maintenance of public order and that the Union government has the duty to protect the states against internal disturbances. A holistic national security policy and the mechanisms for its administration must be urgently finalized in consultation with the states. The Centre must not lose any more time in evolving the required Centre–state understandings for effective national security management.

vi) Apart from finalizing the national security policy, the Central government needs to take time-bound steps to establish appropriate institutions/agencies for effective security management across the length and breadth of the country. It must enact laws and establish all the required processes and procedures for the prompt investigation and trial of federal offences; and it has to establish a national security administrative service for manning and operating the security management apparatus in the entire country.

If the security, unity and integrity of India are to be preserved and protected, there is no more time to be lost. The Central and the state governments must immediately forge all required agreements and take every necessary step for ensuring that there is not the slightest chink in the enforcement of national security.

4

Police and National Security Management*

Under the Indian Constitution, the states have the responsibility of maintaining law and order in their respective jurisdictions. But they may seek the Centre's assistance whenever a serious situation arises, which they are unable to tackle by fully utilizing their available resources. In such circumstances the Centre may deploy its police forces and or the army in aid of civil power (Item 2A, List I, Seventh Schedule). Such deployments of Central armed forces are for specific periods or till such time as a given disorder is brought under control and normalcy is restored.

The Constitution provides that it shall be the duty of the Union to protect the states against external aggression and internal disturbance and to ensure that the government of every state is carried on in accordance with the Constitutional provisions (Article 355). To maintain the federal solidarity, the Union is empowered to issue necessary directions to the states (Articles 256–57) and president's rule can be imposed if there is a failure of constitutional functioning in a state.

Under the original provisions in Article 352, it was stipulated that if the president is satisfied that a grave emergency exists whereby the

* Col Pyara Lal Memorial Lecture, delivered at USI of India, New Delhi, on 20 September 2001 and published in the *USI Journal*. Excerpts.

security of India or any part of the territory thereof is threatened, whether by war or external aggression or internal disturbance, or if there is the imminent danger of such an eventuality, he may enforce emergency in the whole or any part of the country. However, the term 'internal disturbance' was substituted with 'armed rebellion' by the Forty-fourth Amendment (Act 1978). As a result, the Union government can only act in situations of armed rebellion and not merely in the event of outbreak of disorder or disruption of settled conditions. This amendment, I think, has resulted in seriously restricting the Union's authority.

The Constitution also provides for the enforcement of martial law. There has been no occasion in the past for this constitutional provision being put to use.

For discharging their constitutional responsibility to maintain public order in their jurisdictions, the states are expected to maintain adequately trained and equipped police forces. Briefly, the entire civil police administration in the states, from the village level upwards, is expected to gather intelligence, enforce laws, take pre-emptive action to ensure against any disruption of peace and public order, apprehend offenders, investigate cases, launch prosecutions and take every necessary measure to maintain law and order.

The state units of armed police are also expected to assist the district police whenever a situation arises which the latter cannot handle with their own resources. Armed police contingents may also be deployed to manage state-wide agitations or any other larger-scale situation which has the potential of disrupting law and order.

As the essential responsibility for the maintenance of peace and public order rests with the states, it would be useful to examine whether they have equipped themselves to discharge this vital obligation. In this context it may be mentioned that when the founding fathers of our Constitution decided to vest this responsibility in the states, the maintenance of public order largely involved keeping criminal activities under control, making preventive arrests or imposing curfew if the emerging situation so warranted.

Today, the ground reality has undergone a sea change. For the past few decades and more, the police has been required to deal with the serious disorders created by highly motivated and trained insurgent and terrorist groups, which possess unlimited resources, state-of-the-art communication systems, weaponry and remote control gadgetry for causing death and destruction. The state police forces do not possess the required capability and resources to tackle insurgencies, much less the well-organized terrorist groups. The serious deficiencies from which the state police suffer were exposed in the early 1980s when Punjab was faced with Pakistan-supported militancy. The continuing insurgencies in the north-eastern region and Pakistan's proxy war in J&K have further demonstrated the incapacities of the state police organizations.

At the time of Independence, the total strength of the civil and armed police constabularies in the country was less than one lakh. As per the latest available data, the strength of such forces has risen to over fourteen lakh of which, significantly, the total strength of the armed police is merely 3.71 lakh.

Almost every state suffers from acute deficiencies in the strength and infrastructural resources of its civil police set-up. The police stations, grossly understaffed and ill-equipped, cannot be expected to gather intelligence in time or effectively police the areas under their charge. The strength of the armed police maintained by the states is altogether inadequate and far too ill-equipped to tackle in time any arising situation.

Over the years, successive governments in the states, irrespective of their political orientation, have failed to discharge their vital obligation to maintain well-trained, fully equipped and professionally trustworthy civil and armed police forces. Inadequate budgetary support for the police department and the consequentially increasing deficiencies in almost every aspect of police functioning have led to a situation in which the states perpetually call upon the

Union home ministry to deploy Central police forces for tackling virtually every kind of internal disorder.

As a result, the Centre has been compelled to continually increase the strength of the Central police forces, which, in 1999, comprised about 5.9 lakh personnel constituting 354 battalions. While this strength may appear significant, it includes about 220 battalions of forces guarding the border, which should normally never be moved away from the frontiers. It must be noted that the Centre, whenever called upon to deal with serious internal security situations, has had no choice except to withdraw the BSF, ITBP and AR from their mandated roles for indefinite periods. As the Central police forces are themselves not fully trained and equipped to deal with war-like situations, the Centre has also had to deploy the army in aid of civil power on several occasions.

The internal discipline, morale and commitment of any uniformed force is crucially determined by the manner in which it is controlled and managed. Studies undertaken by the Bureau of Police Research and Development in regard to the living and working conditions of the state police forces and various other available reports reveal a most alarming situation:

- Twenty-five per cent of the police stations and 50 per cent of the police outposts do not have regular buildings.
- Over 37 per cent police districts work from makeshift police lines.
- Over 70 per cent police districts do not have a proper control room.
- Superintendents of police in over 34 per cent police districts are not provided residential accommodation.
- Seventy per cent of the constabulary is without residential accommodation.
- The mobility deficiency is approximately 43 per cent.
- The weaponry available with the police is insufficient and obsolete.

- The communication systems are inadequate, out of date and non-functional in most cases.
- The National Police Commission (NPC) had assessed, over twenty years ago, that the constables were required to work an average of thirteen hours a day. Presently, they perform daily duties for even longer hours.
- Police personnel are provided training opportunities only once in twenty years though they are required to undergo training every five years.
- The curricula for the training of policemen, which requires continuing orientation to modern policing practices with special reference to the emerging crime patterns, have not been regularly reviewed and changed.
- Inadequate attention has been paid to the maintenance of up-to-date crime records and communication systems which would enable rapid access and retrieval of the required information for investigating crime.
- Forensic science laboratories are very few in number and even these are inadequately equipped. The speed and quality of investigations are seriously impaired as thousands of references made by the police remain pending for prolonged periods, resulting in the failure of prosecutions and continued resort to obsolete investigative methodologies.

In 1999–2000, the all-India expenditure to maintain police forces with a strength of over fourteen lakh, was no more than Rs 14,922 crore. These figures would readily indicate the impoverished status of the state police organizations. The Bureau of Police Research and Development had estimated in 2000 that an investment of over Rs 30,000 crore would be required to remedy the essential deficiencies in the state police organization.

The experience of dealing with the period of serious disorder in Punjab, the insurgencies in the Northeast, the continuing proxy war in J&K and significant disturbances elsewhere in the country has demonstrated that some of these disturbances may not have escalated into grave internal security problems if they had been promptly and effectively dealt with at the incipient stages.

While prolonged neglect has led to the existing inadequacies of the state police organizations, a factor which has seriously impaired their performance is the persistent interference in their functioning by political and extra-constitutional elements. As the police is among the most visible instruments of the national administrative apparatus, its failure to effectively enforce the law has seriously eroded the image of governance and also created the impression that lawless elements can indulge in criminality with impunity.

It would not be an exaggeration to say that internal security cannot be maintained unless the state police organizations are enabled to function with efficiency, speed and total reliability. This can happen only if immediate measures are taken to systematically remedy each factor which has contributed to the progressive decline in the functioning of the police. Inter alia, besides providing the required financial allocations, the state chief ministers would have to ensure that there is no political interference whatsoever in the day-to-day functioning of the police, especially in regard to recruitments, transfers, postings and promotions of the personnel at all levels. Further, the police would be able to resolve many of their internal problems if the state governments could ensure that all appointments to the senior echelons, especially those of the state police chiefs, are from among officers of proven professional standing and known integrity. For restoring the command-and-control systems, discipline, efficiency and loyalty of the police, it would also be necessary to ensure that all incompetent and dishonest elements are ruthlessly weeded out.

5

Reforming the Police Administration[*]

Sometime ago, a public interest legislation (PIL) was filed in the Supreme Court by two retired police officers. Recalling the major police failures in the past, and attributing them to growing political and bureaucratic interference, the PIL sought the apex court's intervention to issue appropriate directions to the government to redefine the role and function of the police; frame a new Police Act on the lines of the draft bill recommended by the National Police Commission (NPC), and lay down procedures for the selection and appointment of the chiefs of Central and state police organizations, with a minimum statutory tenure (Prakash Singh and others v/s Union of India, 1996).

Problems arising from the decline in the functioning of the state police – and other wings of government – have been known to the Centre for years. The NPC was set up in November 1977 to undertake a comprehensive review of all aspects of the police system in the country. It submitted eight reports during 1979–81. While forwarding its first report to the government, the NPC recorded its deep concern about the increasing intensity of public complaints regarding the oppressive behaviour and excesses by the police and its inability to deal with law and order situations and crime in the country. This report, dealing with the working and living conditions

---

[*] First published in *Hindustan Times*, 11 August 1996.

of the constabulary, was discussed in the conference of chief ministers in 1979 and the states agreed to implement the principal recommendations. Reports II–VIII were discussed by the Cabinet in early 1983 and the government approved that these be released.

The repudiated text of the NPC reports, which apparently caused offence to the government, contained references to the misuse of the police during the Emergency (1975–77) for subverting lawful procedures and serving purely political ends; intelligence organizations being misused for collecting information on political parties and individuals; the decline in the political executive, leading to interference and extraneous pressures being exerted; growth of vested interests and the police being used to put down political dissent; the police openly cultivating politicians and conviction evolving among the personnel that their careers did not depend upon their professional performance; the infringement of command-and-control structures through interference; development of a mala fide nexus between the police and politicians, leading to collusive corruption; and the general public impression that the police is meant to serve only elite groups who can get their jobs done through pressure or bribes.

The Centre forwarded these seven reports to the states in March 1983, requesting them to take appropriate action. Subsequently criticism has been repeatedly voiced that the NPC's reports have been collecting dust in the home ministry and the Centre is unwilling to implement the recommendations. This is not correct. The MHA's view has been that as police is a 'state subject', the Centre can only motivate the states to implement the recommendations and provide necessary guidance. However, a considerable number of the recommendations which fell within the Centre's realm were accepted and many of them have been implemented.

In all, the MHA identified about 140 major recommendations. Of these, about fifty-five required implementation by the states and the remainder concerned the Centre. The MHA has already implemented a number of the recommendations. During the last decade and a half progress has been achieved in regard to police housing, modernization of mechanisms, welfare programmes for personnel, improvement in the wage structure of the constabulary and training of the middle and lower echelons of the state police forces.

However, the recommended amendments to the IPC, Evidence Act and Criminal Procedure Code for the improvement of the criminal justice system have still to receive legislative approval; a decision has still to be taken whether there should be two Central IPS cadres – one for manning the Central paramilitary organizations and the other for providing officers to manage the Intelligence Bureau, RAW and CBI. Another crucial recommendation related to the amendment of Article 311 of the Constitution for weeding out corrupt officers. This matter, referred by MHA to the personnel department, also continues to await a decision.

The states have also implemented a number of the NPC's recommendations. However, they have shown consistent resolve in not accepting the most important among them. A seminal recommendation was for every state to establish a Statutory Security Commission (SSC) headed by the state minister incharge of police and comprising two MLAs, one from the ruling party and another from among the opposition parties, appointed on the advice of the Assembly Speaker; four members to be appointed by the chief minister, subject to the approval of the state legislature, from among retired high court judges, retired senior civil servants, and eminent social scientists or academicians. The state police chief would be the ex-officio secretary of the SSC, which would function on the lines of the state Public Service Commission (PSC).

Another important recommendation relates to the appointment of chiefs of state police organizations. The NPC has recommended that this appointment should be from a panel of not more than three IPS officers of the state cadre. The panel would be prepared by a committee headed by the chairman of the Union Public Service Commission (UPSC) and comprise the Union home secretary, the senior-most among the chiefs of the Central police organizations, the state chief secretary and the outgoing state police chief. Appointments from this panel would be in accordance with seniority. To restore the capacity of the police to resist political interference, extraneous pressures and illegal orders, the NPC recommended a statutory tenure of four years or up to the date of retirement or next promotion. The premature removal of the police chief would require the prior approval of the SSC, except when the incumbent has been awarded a punishment. Further, any officer who has served as the state police chief shall, on retirement, be debarred from re-employment under the state or Central governments or in any state/Central public undertaking.

The NPC also made comprehensive recommendations regarding the strict enforcement of discipline and conduct rules, and ruthless weeding out of corrupt personnel. It also recommended that the head of the state vigilance or anti-corruption bureau should be selected from a panel prepared by a committee headed by the chairman, Central Vigilance Commission (CVC). Needless to say, the state governments have not agreed to such an approach.

Arising from all their recommendations for the reform and effective functioning of the state police forces, the NPC recommended the draft of a new Police Act to replace the Police Act, 1861. As regards the role of the Centre in the policing of the country, the NPC recommended the establishment of an expert, high-powered Central Police Committee (CPC).

As regards the NPC's recommendations in respect of the mode of appointment and tenure of chiefs of state police and vigilance/anti-corruption bureaux and the establishment of state security commissions, no state government has agreed to fall in line. All chief ministers, even the senior-most and seasoned among them, have been taking the position that as law and order is a state subject, the selection and appointment of police officers is the prerogative of the state government and its authority in the matter should not be interfered with. Likewise, it has been argued by state governments that the establishment of a State Security Commission will dilute the state government's control over the police and adversely affect their ability to maintain law and order. As far as the appointments of chief of the state vigilance/anti-corruption bureaux are concerned, most state governments have not offered any clear response.

Regarding the enactment of a new Police Act, on the lines of the draft bill recommended by the NPC, the Centre's position so far, based on legal advice, has been that it is not constitutionally empowered to embark upon such an initiative, as police is part of the State List. It is a moot point whether the proposed bill could ever be enacted even if the Centre suffered no constitutional constraint.

It is a matter for consideration whether the functioning of the state police can be transformed merely by enacting a new Police Act, protecting the topmost police officers by granting them mandatory tenures and expecting that the political executive in the states will overnight give up their unwholesome interests as soon as the state security commissions are set up. Needless to say, no organization which interfaces with the people at large can remain impervious to the obtaining social and moral environment.

POSTSCRIPT

The PIL referred to at the beginning of this chapter remained under process for nearly ten years. In September 2006, the Supreme Court passed a detailed order in which it gave clear directions to the Government of India and the states regarding the implementation of Police Reforms. The Supreme Court directed that:

- State Security Commissions (SSC) shall be established, with members from the government, judiciary and civil society, to evolve policies for ensuring that the 'State Government does not exercise unwanted influence or pressure on the State Police'; the SSC would lay down broad policy guidelines, evaluate the performance of the state police and, overall, act as a watchdog on its functioning;

- The DGP shall be appointed through a transparent and merit-based process and enjoy a minimum tenure of two years;
- Police officers on operational duties (SPs in charge of districts and SHOs in charge of police stations) shall have a minimum tenure of two years;
- The state police establishment board shall be set up to: (i) decide the transfers, postings and other service related matters of police officers of and below the rank of DySP and (ii) make recommendations in regard to the postings and transfers of officers above the rank of DySP;
- The investigation and law and order functions of the police would be separated;
- Police complaint authorities would be set up at the state and district levels to inquire into public complaints against police officers in all cases of serious misconducts;
- A National Security Commission (NSC) would be set up by the Government of India to prepare panels for the selection and appointment of the chiefs of Central police organizations, each of whom shall have a minimum tenure of two years.

Several state governments filed review petitions against the Supreme Court's order, all of which were rejected. Consequently, in the past over nine years since the Supreme Court gave its directions, seventeen states are reported to have introduced new Police Acts. However, from all accounts, it is apparent that all the states remain determined to retain political control over the police and all manner of excuses have been made for circumventing the Supreme Court's directions which were passed after several years of consideration.

Over seven years ago, in May 2008, the Supreme Court set up a monitoring committee to review and oversee the implementation of its directions to the states. This committee, headed by Justice K.T. Thomas, a retired Supreme Court judge, reported that practically no state had fully complied with the apex court's directions in letter and spirit. Among the specious reasons given by certain states for non-implementation were:

- That the Supreme Court had not given any 'directions' but only made certain 'recommendations';
- That the executive authority of the state is vested in the governor who shall act in accordance with the aid and advice of the council of ministers or the Cabinet (Articles 154 and 163);
- That the court has no power to enquire whether any, and if so what advice was tendered to the governor [Article 163(3)].

It is a matter of concern that the Centre has also not effectively implemented the envisaged role of the National Security Commission nor finalized the Model Police Act of which a draft was prepared nearly a decade ago, by a committee chaired by a former attorney general.

6

Overlapping Authority*

The states have developed an unfortunate proclivity to invoke the assistance of the army to deal with situations which, in many cases, could have been adequately managed by their armed police forces, assisted, as necessary, by the central paramilitary forces (CPMF). In recent years, most of the states have found it convenient to pass on their problems to the Centre. From their perspective it would appear that the armed forces of the Union were essentially created to bridge the gaps arising from the failure of the states to discharge their constitutional responsibility!

At the time of Independence there was only one Central police force of limited strength, the Central Reserve Police Force (CRPF), which was meant for providing occasional support to the states for the maintenance of law and order. The only other armed force bequeathed by the British was the Assam Rifles (AR), which was essentially an ethnic force for operations in the Northeast under the command and control of the army. From the 1960s onwards, a number of new CPMF were created: the Border Security Force (BSF, for guarding the western borders in the plains); the Indo-Tibetan Border Police (ITBP, for guarding the Himalayan frontiers); the Railway Protection Force (RPF, for providing security to the Railways); the Central Industrial Security Force (CISF, for the security

---

* First published in *Hindustan Times*, 9 April 1996.

of the Central public sector undertakings); the National Security Guards (NSG, for commando, anti-hijacking, etc., operations); and the Special Protection Group (SPG, for VIP security duties).

In the past, under increasing pressure from the states, the home ministry has been deploying sizeable elements of any of its available forces for performing internal security duties all over the country, virtually on an uninterrupted basis. Except for the CRPF, which is the only Central police force trained to provide support to the states for the maintenance of law and order, the ad hoc deployment of other CPMF for internal security duties has been at significant cost to their mandated roles. This has also adversely affected their training and has left the CPMF personnel – pushed around from state to state and denied leave – exhausted and demoralized.

It is essentially the responsibility of the states to ensure the orderly conduct of polls, whenever held. In earlier years, the Centre used to provide marginal support, through deployment of CRPF, to ensure peaceful elections in identified sensitive areas. Over time, with the state police forces acquiring a reputation for being communally inclined and being generally viewed as undependable, the Election Commission of India has been compelling the home ministry to ensure heavy deployment of CPMF in all states facing elections. Thus, for one or the other reason, nearly half the total strength of the CPMF, and at times more, remains permanently deployed in support of the states, neglecting the tasks for which these forces were raised.

To deal with insurgency and terrorism the Centre has been compelled, in the past, to also deploy the army. Such deployment in Punjab and the Northeast, and for the last decade and more in J&K, has adversely affected the army's training and preparedness. This involvement has also resulted in army personnel facing charges of atrocities, theft, loot, torture, infringing human rights, etc., and consequent inquiries, litigation and public criticism. Similar problems have also been faced by the CPMF personnel deployed for tackling difficult problems.

There is a general perception that the responsibility for national security management essentially involves the defence and home ministries. While the defence ministry continues to remain answerable for external security, i.e., national defence, it is a moot point whether the home ministry has the requisite authority and is suitably equipped for effectively managing internal security.

In the past, the home ministry controlled the functioning of the all-India services – the Indian Administrative Service (IAS) and the Indian Police Service (IPS) – and, in this process, was able to exercise considerable influence over the states in all matters relating to internal security management. Also, till about the early 1970s, the same political party ruled most of the states and at the Centre and the former generally looked to the latter for advice and direction. Later, with changes in the political scene in the various states and Centre–state relations developing new perspectives, there has been a progressive decline in the Centre's influence.

There has also been progressive dilution of the home ministry's inherent authority. It no longer manages the IAS cadre or controls the functioning of the Central Bureau of Investigation; both are in a department under the prime minister's charge. The home ministry does not even have full control over the management of the IPS cadre! Both the external intelligence agency and the Joint Intelligence Committee are under the Cabinet secretariat, under the prime minister. Consequently, the home ministry is left looking after immigration and internal intelligence, with a highly fractured responsibility for the management of the IPS.

The problem does not end there. There are many other major departments and agencies of the Centre, under various ministries, whose functioning inherently involves dealing with issues which have high security significance. For example, banking, revenue intelligence, income tax, customs, enforcement directorate, narcotics, coastguard, etc., are under the Ministry of Finance and the various governmental and autonomous agencies – Directorate General of Civil Aviation, International Airports Authority of

India, National Airports Authority, Civil Aviation Security, etc. – which are responsible for controlling the movements of domestic and foreign aircraft in our national airspace and at our airports function under the Ministry of Civil Aviation.

These and many other agencies which have a role in the maintenance of national security, operate within their administrative ethos and are answerable only to their controlling ministries. Thus, the best endeavours of the home ministry get confined to seeking the cooperation of each of the various organizations outside its control. These efforts to secure coordination consume considerable time and energy. Furthermore, the responses of the agencies whose support is solicited are not always prompt and wholesome. Intelligence, at times even information, is not timely and fully shared. As has happened many times in the past, the required support may become available far too late, if at all.

The grave hazard of the home ministry continuing to manage national security through 'coordination' was amply demonstrated in December 1995 when a foreign aircraft paradropped arms and ammunition in Purulia (see Appendix 2) and made several unauthorized landings at Indian airports before being apprehended, virtually perchance. Though several years have since elapsed, the investigations have not as yet been able to even identify those for whom the munitions were meant!

The serious security problems which obtain in several parts of the country and the Purulia incident have made it abundantly clear that the existing structures for security management are inadequate and that the 'coordination' approach is an obsolete idea.

7

Autonomous by Default*

While national security management involves a host of issues, perhaps the most important single factor relates to the timely procurement of valid intelligence and its prompt and effective utilization. In earlier years the Intelligence Bureau (IB) was responsible for both internal and external intelligence. In the late 1960s, external intelligence was entrusted to the Research and Analysis Wing (RAW), an agency under the Cabinet secretariat, reporting to the prime minister.

Over the years the IB's functioning has undergone significant changes. Till the time of Home Minister Y.B. Chavan, it was an integral part of the Ministry of Home Affairs (MHA) and functioned under the control and direction of the home minister (HM). However, when Indira Gandhi, impelled by power politics, weakened the HM's role, the director of the IB (DIB) was asked to report directly to the prime minister on certain matters. From then on, successive DIBs did not find it obligatory to look to the HM for direction and control. The continuing decline of the MHA's role in governance provided further impetus to DIBs taking their own decisions about who had to be informed about what, and to what extent. The appointment, from time to time, of ministers of state with independent charge of internal security further weakened the

* First published in *The Indian Express*, 30 January 1997.

HM's authority and virtually legalized the DIB's ignoring him. The short tenures of HMs, some of whom did not have the background needed to effectively oversee and direct the IB, caused further deterioration.

If the HM was not an altogether relevant factor for the IB, the home secretary (HS) obviously did not deserve to be noticed. This was accentuated by the quick turnover of HSs, some of whom, like their ministers, had very little justification for their appointments. The only occasion on which the DIB is compelled to recognize the HS is when he needs from the latter an annual certificate that the IB's secret fund was usefully spent under the HS's 'directions'. For want of support from higher quarters, successive HSs have meekly issued this certificate, which is forwarded to the Comptroller and Auditor General (CAG), which – as per arrangement with this constitutional authority – exempts the IB from scrutiny.

The IB has emerged as a virtually independent agency except for seeking certain sanctions from the MHA – when the DIB travels abroad, his officers are seconded to assignments at home or abroad. In the absence of a mechanism to evaluate the quality of intelligence generated by the IB, its contribution and usefulness in national security management has largely depended on the professional competence of those appointed as DIB, some of them outstanding officers. In the style of functioning established over time, the DIB alone knows what his officers are doing and to what effect.

Let me now go on to the case of Rattan Sehgal. According to published reports, this 'hard core' IB officer (he belonged to the permanent cadre of the IB), heading the counter-espionage division in the IB, was found indulging in unauthorized, frequent contacts with two locally based CIA (Central Intelligence Agency) operatives. He did not keep the DIB informed of the need for, or outcome of, these contacts. He was observed accepting a 'packet' from one of the CIA agents and his office and home were searched but nothing incriminating was discovered. He was also subjected to exhaustive questioning after which he was given the option of resigning or face removal from service. He sought retirement and he was allowed to retire. The US ambassador was asked to ensure that the CIA operatives left the country 'quietly'. The matter was reviewed by a group comprising the cabinet secretary, home secretary, foreign secretary, DIB and secretary (RAW).

In an interview, the HM admitted that the Sehgal affair was a 'serious' matter, that investigations were in progress and that the case had not been closed. It is a matter of the most serious concern that one of the senior-most IB officers, hand-picked for heading the counter-espionage wing, was compelled to quit service for serious deviations from the norm. Anxiety heightens when one recalls that this is not the first case of its kind. A few years ago a senior naval officer, serving at the Indian embassy in Islamabad, had to be dismissed under the National Security Act on discovery that he had been compromised by Pakistani intelligence. As for the CIA's activities in India, in the early 1990s the then DIB had reported that a CIA operative – who had attempted to infiltrate the IB – was extradited, also 'quietly'.

Consequent to the intermeshing of internal and external security issues, it is of crucial importance that IB and RAW function in an orderly and productive manner, maintaining close and effective coordination. At present, there is no mechanism to assess the productivity of our two apex intelligence agencies. The Purulia incident exposed the most alarming inadequacy of the existing arrangements. The Sehgal episode is another reminder that there is much to worry about.

Faced with complex and serious problems, the government has a tendency to seek quick, ad hoc and convenient solutions. Such an approach cannot any longer apply. The MHA has not prescribed the IB's role for years. There must be no further delay in promulgating the IB's charter of duties and responsibilities, especially prescribing its channel of reporting. RAW's role has also changed in recent years. Its charter needs to be reviewed and redefined, specially laying down its interface with the IB. These issues will not be resolved unless the home minister and prime minister feel adequately concerned. Dithering could have the most serious consequences.

8

Security in the Indian Ocean[*]

The Indian Ocean was the first centre of maritime activity in the world. Civilization took birth around its waters over 5,000 years ago. The civilizations of Nineveh and Babylon had links with the western coast of present-day India; the monsoon winds facilitated long voyages across the ocean.

The earliest record of Indian maritime activity appears in the literature of the Vedic period (2000–500 BC). The motto of the Indian Navy, 'Çam No Varunah' (Sam no Varunah) meaning 'May the Lord of the Oceans be auspicious unto us', for instance, dates back to this period. It is an invocation (in Sanskrit) to Lord Varuna, the Lord of the Sea.

Before we discuss security in the Indian Ocean Region (IOR) we must have a view about its geographical limits and the area it encompasses. And here we find considerable confusion and differences in perception. The term Indian Ocean 'rim' refers to both littoral and island states and their number varies from a low of twenty-eight to a high of thirty-five – the latter comprising twenty-nine littoral and six island states. At the meeting of the International Forum on the Indian Ocean Region (IFIOR) held

---

[*] First published in Air Commodore Jasjit Singh (ed.), *Bridges Across the Indian Ocean*, New Delhi: Institute for Defence Studies and Analyses, 1997.

in Perth in June 1995, only twenty-eight rim countries (including island states) were invited.

The term 'region' is understood to refer to both the rim and the hinterland states; the latter being those dependent on the Indian Ocean. Even here, the numbers vary from forty-seven to fifty-two, if the five Central Asian Republics (CARs) are included. Meanwhile, the Indian Ocean 'community' could be stated to comprise as many as sixty states, including those not even remotely connected to the Indian Ocean!

A major feature of the IOR is the sheer diversity amongst its countries. This relates to their size (Australia vis-a-vis Singapore), their populations (India's 950 million people vis-a-vis 72,000 in Seychelles), and the nature of their political systems. Sharp variations exist in the levels of economic development – countries whose gross domestic product (GDP) varies from US$293.6 billion (India) to US$1.5 billion (Mozambique), and variations in gross national product (GNP) per capita from US$22,500 (Singapore) to US$90 (Mozambique). The IOR also includes a number of very weak economies, as well as the fastest-growing ones of South-east Asia. All the countries of the region are categorized as developing states, with the exception of Australia and Israel. The population of the IOR is over a third of the world's population.

The IOR possesses vast natural resources, both mineral and marine. Two-thirds of the world's total proven reserves of natural gas are located here. The oil reserves of the Persian Gulf are expected to last for over a century for Kuwait, the UAE and Iraq; and eighty-five years for Saudi Arabia. The gas reserves of the IOR are expected to last for over 100 years. Huge deposits of a number of other mineral resources such as gold, diamond and uranium are also found in the region. It is estimated that 40 per cent of gold, 90 per cent of diamond and 60 per cent of uranium deposits worldwide are located in the IOR.

TRADE AND SEA LINES OF COMMUNICATION IN THE INDIAN OCEAN

The importance of the IOR also lies in its geographical location and its strategic waterways – the latter providing the shortest and most economical lines of communication between the Atlantic and the Pacific oceans. Therefore, it is not surprising that, according to one estimate, the Indian Ocean accounts for the transportation of the highest tonnage of goods in the world. The vast majority of this trade is extra-regional by nature, with intra-regional trade accounting for only 20 per cent of total Indian Ocean trade. This is in marked contrast to the Asia-Pacific economies around the Pacific Ocean, where intra-regional trade accounts for as much as 66 per cent of the total trade.

In terms of trade, the IOR is one of the fastest-growing areas in the world. Its total trade was estimated at US$957.6 billion in 1994 as against US$526.3 billion in 1988. Although the region traditionally has had an adverse balance of trade with the rest of the world, the size of the trade deficit is progressively receding. While the exports of the region were increasing at the rate of 13.7 per cent per annum, the growth rate for imports was 13.6 per cent during 1988–94. The share of the region in world trade was 9.6 per cent in 1988, and rose to 13.6 per cent in 1994.

The physical characteristics of the Indian Ocean – it is virtually surrounded by land on three sides – enhance the importance of its strategic waterways. The most important among these waterways in the western part of the IOR include the Suez Canal (which connects the Red Sea to the Mediterranean Sea) and the Strait of Hormuz (which links the Persian Gulf to the Gulf of Oman); in the eastern part of the IOR, the Straits of Malacca, Singapore, Sunda and Lombak provide critical links with the Pacific Ocean.

DIMENSIONS OF NON-MILITARY SECURITY

Energy Vulnerability

The Strait of Hormuz is, by far, the single most important waterway in the Indian Ocean, accounting for the movement of a high proportion of energy supplies and other commodities of trade. The oil and natural gas from the Persian Gulf are supplied to countries of the Indian, Atlantic and Pacific oceans which are dependent on these supplies for their economic growth and prosperity. In this respect, the Strait of Hormuz accounts for over 33 per cent of global imports of crude oil annually.

The dependence of various countries on the supply of crude oil from the Persian Gulf is likely to increase considerably in the near future. This would be due to their growing demand for oil, shortfall in the rate of domestic production, and declining reserves. In view of the fast-paced economic growth rates and industrialization of the eastern sector of the IOR, its demand for energy is expected to increase annually at a rate higher than that of the global demand. The demand for crude oil in the Asia-Pacific Region (APR), for example, is expected to grow at a rate of 3.0–5.5 per cent annually. This increase will account for nearly two-thirds of total expected volume growth in the world oil market between 1992–93 and 2004–05. Thus, with crude oil production being unable to keep pace with demand, the region's dependency on the import of oil, especially from the Persian Gulf, is expected to increase substantially. In this respect, it is estimated that the region's share of crude oil imported from the Persian Gulf will dramatically increase by 2005. The security of the importing countries shall be seriously affected if they do not receive uninterrupted supplies of crude oil.

Proliferation of Small Arms and the Spread of Narcotics

Another critical dimension of non-military security is the growing proliferation of small arms and the spread of the narcotics menace. These problems, of increasing concern to the IOR countries, generate tensions in the area and spread a form of warfare which is being witnessed worldwide. The term 'small arms/light weapons' is highly misleading, and often tends to generate a misplaced sense of complacency among strategic analysts. Small arms are quite clearly no longer 'small' in lethality, range, accuracy or effect. In North Atlantic Treaty Organization (NATO) terminology, for instance, these weapons embrace all crew-portable direct fire weapons of a calibre less than 50 mm, and include a secondary capability to defeat light armour and helicopters.

The so-called small arms comprise landmines, automatic assault rifles, rocket-propelled grenade launchers, shoulder-fired surface-to-air missiles, and high explosives. In terms of the spread of landmines, for example, nearly 110 million of these weapons are deployed in more than sixty countries. Of the nine most seriously affected countries, six (Afghanistan, Iraq, Kuwait, Mozambique, Somalia and Sudan) are located in the IOR. Furthermore, 500 million guns are believed to be in circulation in the world, including fifty-five million Kalashnikov automatic assault rifles. Some 1.5 million AK-47 rifles are stated to be unaccounted for in the IOR state of Mozambique alone. With such developments, it is not surprising that non-state actors in many of these countries are increasingly challenging the structure and institutions of the state.

In view of the nature of the war fought against the erstwhile Soviet Union in Afghanistan during the 1980s, the vast quantities of weapons supplied to the mujahidin forces were of the small arms variety. Over the years, a large proportion of these weapons, diverted within Pakistan itself, have been used in the Indian states of Punjab and Jammu and Kashmir. During the seven-year period, from mid-1988 to mid-1995, the weapons and ammunition seized by the Indian security forces in J&K included 13,894 AK series assault rifles, 844 machine guns, 601 rocket launchers, 1,667 rockets, nearly 5,000 pistols/revolvers, over two million rounds of assorted ammunition, and 8,622 kg of explosives. Some of these arms, transported across the sea and off-loaded on the west Indian coast, were used in organizing bomb blasts in Bombay in 1993.

This state of affairs is further exacerbated by the nexus between the arms suppliers and the production and trade in narcotics in the area, resulting in narco-terrorism. All the three countries comprising the world's largest drug-growing area, the Golden Crescent, are in the IOR: Pakistan, Afghanistan and Iran. To make matters worse, Myanmar and Thailand, two of the three countries of another vast drug-producing area, the Golden Triangle, are also in the IOR. The cultivation and trafficking of drugs encourage the establishment of well-funded private armies, as witnessed in Afghanistan, Pakistan and Myanmar, as well as covert channels of distribution. The drug trade generates enormous funds for the purchase of sophisticated small arms which are distributed amongst militant groups in the area who use them to create terrorism and disruption.

Human Security

Yet another dimension of non-military security, not often discussed, relates to the serious insecurities which emanate from under-development and grossly imbalanced development of nation states. This aspect, of human security, specially concerns a large number of countries in the IOR which, after long years of colonial rule and exploitation, have still to achieve, even approximately, the desired standards of human development. Thus, when we talk of security in the countries of the IOR, we must, of necessity, reckon with the tensions inherent in underdeveloped and developing societies as these have high potential of being exploited by elements within and outside the country.

INDIA'S POLICIES

A look at the world map will illustrate the importance of the Indian Ocean, and the states of its region, to India's foreign policy. Geographically situated at the centre of an inverted arc, the IOR comprises India's strategic neighbourhood. Within this area, India is by far the most populous state, sharing territorial and maritime boundaries with ten other countries. In view of its location, India lies astride the major sea lines of communication in the ocean, thereby providing it considerable geostrategic importance. These factors provide India considerable scope to play a proactive and useful role in the IOR.

In the past, India has contributed to the maintenance of peace and security in the IOR and remains firmly committed to do so in the future. India's help, on occasion, has been in the form of support to the democratic governments of smaller states in the region, as was the case of India's role in Sri Lanka and the Maldives in the late 1980s. In terms of regional cooperation, India follows a consensus-based approach. This is especially so in the case of the Indian Ocean Rim Initiative, formally inaugurated as the Indian Ocean Rim Association for Regional Cooperation (IOR-ARC) in Mauritius in March 1997.

In terms of the charter of the IOR-ARC, a fundamental principle is that decisions on all matters and issues and at all levels are to be taken on the basis of consensus. In addition, bilateral and other issues likely to generate controversy, and impede regional cooperation, are to be excluded from all deliberations within the Association. This is important, as the basic aim of the Association is to enhance economic cooperation in the Indian Ocean rim primarily through the encouragement of trade and investment.

There has been further reduction in the allocation for defence in the past decade, which has declined from almost 4 per cent of GDP in the late 1980s to 2.3 per cent of GDP in 1996–97. It is a matter of serious concern that while India has been making serious efforts to reduce its defence expenditure, the armed forces have had to be called upon to combat externally supported irregular warfare. India has faced a proxy war in Punjab from the early 1980s, and is continuing to do so in Jammu and Kashmir since the late 1980s. Militancy and terrorism have been supported from across the borders by supply of motivation, training, funds and lethal arms and ammunition. Despite availability of ample evidence of our neighbours' systematic involvement in this proxy war, they have not been discouraged by those who support them for their own interests.

THE REGIONAL MILITARY SECURITY ENVIRONMENT

The end of the cold war and the disintegration of the erstwhile Union of Soviet Socialist Republic (USSR) brought about significant changes in the international security environment. The absence of the USSR and the departure of US military forces from naval and air bases in the Asia–Pacific generated the perception of a 'vacuum' in the area, and threw up various ideas about the countries which might seek to fill it up. A cover story in the *Far Eastern Economic Review* depicted the departure of US and USSR naval forces from the Indian Ocean and suggested that there was competition emerging amongst the navies of India, Japan and China, to exercise control over the area!

Such perceptions continue to be discussed and commented upon by those who have convinced themselves about the 'vacuum' theory. Some of the countries in the region perceive the US presence as one generating stability and thus wish that it would continue. While the United States continues to be the single most powerful country in the world, it also appreciates the limitations in its exercise of military power in the region. Perceptions about the future role of the US in this area are likely to assume greater complexity if the notion of a 'vacuum' in the IOR continues to hold sway, notwithstanding the rationality thereof.

India has considerable maritime interests in the Indian Ocean, which include its growing dependence on the sea for trade, energy resources and the extraction of polymetallic nodules from the seabed in the coming years. India's coastline of over 6,000 km extends deep into the Indian Ocean; the vast expanse of sea on three sides enhances the intensity of the relationship between the land and the sea. This coastline is augmented by about 1,400 km of island and rock territories in the Arabian Sea and the Bay of Bengal. The changes in the international Law of the Sea, formalized in November 1994, support India's claim to an extended maritime zone, including 200 nautical miles of exclusive economic zone (EEZ), which would dramatically increase India's sea area to some 2.8 million sq. km or over two-thirds of the total area of land.

Notwithstanding the nature and extent of these maritime interests, the force level of the Indian Navy has been declining for want of adequate funding and timely decisions. The estimated decrease in the number of principal combatants from 1995 to 2000 would be unprecedented in India's naval history since Independence, accounting for an almost one-third reduction in principal combatants. It is also to be kept in view that, considering India's non-aligned foreign policy, there is no possibility of her entering into military alliances of any kind to reduce the adverse effect of the emerging gap on the naval front.

Japan has a strong and binding security relationship with the United States, and the presence of American military forces on its territory. While Japan's dependence on supplies of oil from the Persian Gulf is expected to increase in the future, the security thereof would be assured by the US–Japan relationship. It is also relevant to note that Japan's expenditure on its self-defence forces is considerable, even though it may represent just above 1 per cent of the country's sizeable GDP.

China may not be a military threat to India's security but it is perceived as a major source of concern to India and to future stability in the region. Such apprehensions emerge from the continuing rapid growth of China's military and economic power. Also, the lessons of the 1962 conflict with China have not been forgotten, especially the high cost India paid for having been caught unprepared. Notwithstanding such memories, India does not seek to contain China or countervail its influence in the region, much less involve itself in such objectives in concert with other countries.

China remains an important neighbour of India and considerable importance is being placed on engaging it constructively. The recent visit of the Chinese president to India saw the conclusion of a number of military-related agreements on confidence-building measures (CBM) between the two countries. This was a natural development of the 1993 Sino-Indian Agreement on Peace and Tranquillity on its borders.

China is developing her interests in the Indian Ocean in terms of trade and as a critical source for its energy requirements. The latter will become increasingly important as China's dependence on crude oil from the Persian Gulf grows. While China's assertive policies in the South China Sea have gained international notice, its increased interest in the seas around India has not been adequately observed. Since the early 1990s, reports have indicated the assistance provided by China for the construction of naval and electronic facilities in Myanmar. These essentially relate to the modernization of the naval base on Hianggyi Island at the mouth of the Bassein river, the construction of a Signals Intelligence (SIGINT) facility on the Great Coco Island, and the development of existing naval infrastructure at Akyab and Mergui.

Chinese activities in the strategically located Coco Islands, which is at a distance of only 20 nautical miles from the Indian Andaman chain of islands, are of concern to India. In 1993, some seventy Chinese naval and technical personnel were believed to have arrived on the island to install new radar equipment. This facility could enable Chinese military personnel to monitor Indian naval communications in the area, and possibly even India's ballistic missile tests off its eastern coast. Further, by 1997, China has provided Myanmar with over $1.6 billion worth of arms. Chinese interests in the region also include important defence ties with Pakistan, Bangladesh and Myanmar. Notwithstanding the end of superpower naval rivalry in the Indian Ocean, the United States, as a global power, continues to maintain critical interests in the area. These include the movement of crude oil and trade through the Persian Gulf and the Indian Ocean, as well as the security of friendly states in the area. The establishment of a permanently deployed independent fleet in 1995, for operations in the north-western Indian Ocean, indicates increased US commitment to the area, and represents a crucial aspect of the US naval doctrine. American military presence in the Indian Ocean has also increased considerably with the new Fifth Fleet off Bahrain in the Persian Gulf, warships of the Seventh Fleet deployed in the central and eastern parts of the Indian Ocean, additional rotationally deployed forces, a major logistics support base at Diego Garcia, and forward-stationed forces in the area.

India has most significantly curtailed spending on defence in the past decade, with serious effects on maintenance and modernization. If resources permit, it may become necessary to devote greater attention to our naval capability as well as to the other two services.

9

Beyond Pokhran and Chagai*

India conducted a fresh series of nuclear tests in May 1998; the first one was conducted in 1974. Within days, Pakistan also conducted similar tests. Long before carrying out these tests, Pakistan had emphatically declared, on several occasions, its nuclear weapon status. One way or another, the events of May 1998 have set at rest any ambiguity about the non-conventional military capability of both the countries, whatever the qualitative differentials be.

Ever since the emergence of India and Pakistan as independent states, the latter has challenged India's territorial integrity on three occasions, in 1947, 1965 and 1971. After the last conflict, a dialogue between the leaders of both the countries led to the conclusion of the Simla Agreement; India agreed to return the captured territories and over 90,000 military personnel of Pakistan. The two neighbours also agreed to maintain peaceful relations, resolving all problems through bilateral negotiations.

The Sino-Indian conflict took place in 1962. China occupied several thousand square kilometres of Indian territory, rejecting the historical demarcation of the boundary between the two countries. Later, Pakistan unauthorizedly ceded to China a sizeable chunk of the territory of Pakistan-occupied Kashmir (PoK).

---

* First published in *The Observer*, August 1998. The United States had imposed sanctions on India after the May 1998 nuclear tests by India.

THE INVISIBLE HAND

Despite the role played by the ISI over the past decades, India has shown sustained patience and adhered to the Simla Pact. India's approach has not yet yielded the envisaged outcome. Domestic politics and the role that the army and ISI play in Pakistan have stood in the way of mutually beneficial solutions being found with regard to most outstanding issues.

While Pakistan has been the victim of its own limited perspective, India too has not displayed any interest in putting aside at least the less intricate security-related problems between the two countries. For instance, by end-1992, both sides had agreed to pull out of the Siachen glacier and demilitarize the area. However, India chose to defer the signing of this accord to early 1993. That day never came. India's approach to the resolution of the Sir Creek and Tulbul issues has not been any more energetic.

As regards China, after nearly two-and-a-half decades of diplomatic stand-off, India launched an initiative in the late 1980s and, following bilateral discussions, the way was cleared to establish mutually agreed mechanisms to maintain 'peace and tranquillity' along the line of actual control (LAC) and for both sides to meet regularly under the aegis of a joint working group. While this approach has still to yield any substantial result in regard to the resolution of the essential issues relating to the boundary, it has contributed to lowering the tensions along the LAC and provided a useful arrangement for dealing with border issues.

THE POKHRAN FALLOUT

After Pokhran II and the Chagai nuclear tests, there has been a significant change in India's security environment. Pakistan, despite its earlier declarations of possessing long-range nuclear missiles which could destroy all major Indian cities, has since been repeatedly stating that it was compelled to conduct nuclear tests because of the imminent threat of a pre-emptive nuclear strike by India in collaborations with Israel; that Kashmir was the core issue between India and Pakistan, which now could be resolved only through third-party intervention; that there was a very high possibility of a nuclear flare-up between the countries at any time, etc.

India has reiterated its commitment to bilaterally resolve all issues, including Kashmir, rejecting outright any third-party involvement, and to conclude a 'no first use' pact with Pakistan and other necessary confidence-building measures. India has indicated its willingness to discuss with the US and others concerned, and also to sign the Comprehensive Test Ban Treaty (CTBT) on certain terms. In the post–Pokhran II phase, India has complained against China's clandestine support to Pakistan's nuclear development programme and to the US playing a partisan role by refusing to take note of the China–Pakistan nexus.

The US has in the past imposed sanctions against both India and Pakistan. The UK, Russia, France, Germany, Sweden, Canada and several other countries which have been supporting India's socio-economic development programmes for many years have also displayed, in varying degrees, unwillingness to keep up the momentum of their erstwhile bilateral support. Japan has displayed greater aggressiveness than many other countries. The stock market has declined, the rupee has witnessed further depreciation and the foreign exchange reserve is not growing at the same rate as in the preceding year. This situation could result in adversely affecting the pace of India's economic development programme.

It is our good fortune that democracy is deeply embedded in India. While the uncertainties in the political scenario may continue for some time, there should be no doubt in any quarter that, notwithstanding which political party rules at the Centre, all necessary measures shall be taken to fully safeguard India's economic and territorial integrity. This, however, should not mean that India may and should meet the existing and emerging challenges merely through strengthening its defence capabilities. Every effort must be made to evolve a practical approach in resolving our problems with Pakistan and China and to bring relations with the US on an even keel. To move in this direction, a conscious effort would have to be made to see that the postures at present taken by China and the US, and by both countries together, are not taken as fixed and final guideposts.

It is far too early to assume that the present Washington–Beijing stance, compelled by trade interests, will be sustained. Arising from its domestic compulsions, China may soon need to review its historical and civilizational linkages with India and other neighbours and seriously reassess whether and to what extent its future role should be engineered by Washington. While the US will seek to sustain its superpower status in a unipolar set-up, the time may not be far off when pressure from Europe and Asia and elsewhere will engender a multi-polar world. India should not commit the mistake of merely reacting to the difficulties in which it is presently mired. It must lake a long-term view and evolve its responses within a wider perspective.

LOOKING AHEAD

Both India and Pakistan face serious problems at home – population, poverty, disease, illiteracy, unemployment and increasing social tensions. It will indeed be a historical blunder if, compelled by the nuclear capability syndrome, they further delay devoting attention to the resolution of the problems which stand between the two countries. Sustained socio-economic development would enable both countries to advance their national goals. This cannot happen if Pakistan continues its proxy war with India and our borders continue to remain tense. Peaceful relations would open the door to mutually profitable trade and business. An arms race, with inescapable high allocations for defence, will spell disaster for both the countries. Pakistan, economically much weaker than India, must keep its future in mind. If it does, India should not be found wanting.

10

Histories of War[*]

The large-scale intrusion into Indian territory, across over 150 km of the Drass–Kargil–Batalik salient, was a Pakistan army operation. The extent to which this venture, meticulously planned by its army chief, was assisted by the mujahidin is a non-issue. The two have been operating together for years and the distinction between 'regular' and 'irregular' has long since been obliterated.

The initial lie, mouthed by the Pakistan foreign minister during his June visit to Delhi, that the intrusion across the line of control was the handwork of 'home-grown revolutionaries' was entirely demolished by General Musharraf's subsequent statements and allegations against the Pakistani prime minister. Exposure of the Kargil-related politico-military web of lies led to the Pakistani army yet again ousting an elected government.

The Pakistan army's intrusion across the LoC was not just another cross-border incident. It was an act of war and the intensity of the bloody battles which followed the aggression could well have led to a prolonged conflict with disastrous consequences for peace in the subcontinent. It was the highly restrained response of the Indian leadership and the subsequent role of the US government which provided Pakistan a face-saving exit.

The Kargil war resulted in over 400 of our brave officers and

* First published in *Hindustan Times*, 11 November 1999.

men being killed and more than twice the number were seriously injured. The almost real-time portrayal of the heroic deeds of our soldiers on television screens generated a wave of national fervour of an unprecedented scale and intensity. It was hoped that this overwhelming expression of solidarity would be consolidated to generate a strong apolitical environment to bring our people closer together and forge a new national spirit. Sadly, this never happened.

Instead, both the ruling and the opposition parties brazenly sought to politically exploit the Kargil card to secure electoral gains. In the process, a golden opportunity to weld the country together was frittered away. Even more unfortunate, the positions taken and statements made sought to politicize the role of our armed forces, cynically disregarding the fact that they have remained a professional, dependable and truly secular wing of the government only because they have so far not been exposed to the vagaries of politics.

A vital concern relating to the Kargil war is how our army was so patently caught on the wrong foot. Was this a failure of the internal and external intelligence agencies or a more comprehensive failure of the army and, consequently, of the entire defence establishment and the government?

The government set up the Subrahmanyam Committee to inquire into the Kargil-related failures. A similar inquiry had been undertaken after the 1962 war. The consequent Henderson Brooks Report, graded Top Secret, has remained classified for over three decades now. While certain corrective actions were taken by the defence ministry to remedy the grave systemic failures brought out in this report, subsequent generations of military officers and defence planners have been denied the opportunity of learning valuable lessons from our past failures.

In the past fifty years, the general approach has been to prevent any substantial discussion on important security-related issues, even in parliament, on the premise that such a debate would not be in the 'national security interest'. Keeping in view the serious security problems that we have faced in the past two decades and the enormous human and economic losses that we continue to suffer, it has become necessary, more than ever before, that the requirements of confidentiality are not allowed to cover lapses, at whatever level they may occur.

To enable the National Security Council to correct the aberrations which may dilute the effective functioning of the defence and security apparatus, it may not be enough for the findings of only the Subrahmanyam Committee to become public. Even at this late stage it would be immensely profitable if the lessons learnt from the 1962, 1965 and 1971 wars were critically reviewed by the Chiefs of Staff Committee and the defence ministry. For such an effort to yield any result, it would be necessary to shed the decades-old cloak of secrecy and lose no more time in most carefully scanning the enormous amount of material which is available with the defence ministry.

The defence ministry used to have a History Division to prepare official histories of major military engagements. The draft histories were prepared after close examination of the operational diaries and all information available in the three service headquarters, the ministries of defence, external affairs and home affairs, the prime minister's office, the Cabinet secretariat and intelligence agencies and interviewing the key civil and military officers who were involved. Unfortunately, faced with an acute financial crunch, the defence ministry was compelled to wind up this division in early 1993.

However, before doing so, we succeeded in finalizing the histories of the 1962, 1965 and 1971 wars despite hesitation in the service headquarters, and the external affairs ministry's traditional view that the sensitive material sought to be published would create problems on various fronts. We resolved the problem by securing the government's approval to remove all footnotes and references to the original sources and bringing out numbered copies of the three histories for restricted internal circulation. The defence-planning structures and all those involved with security management will benefit if these histories are made public without further delay. Histories of the IPKF (Indian Peace-Keeping Force) operations in Sri Lanka and the Kargil war should also be prepared and published early. This would further add to the corpus of post-1947 Indian military history, enlarge the vision of the present and emerging generations of military leaders and contribute to an improved understanding of security-related issues.

11

Managing Security through Fixed Tenures?*

Sometime ago, the Union government amended the relevant rule to provide that those appointed as defence and home secretaries, chiefs of internal and external intelligence agencies, the director of the Central Bureau of Investigation and the cabinet secretary get the required extensions to enjoy two-year tenures. This is to ensure the effective functioning of the security management apparatus. It is not clear why the foreign secretary has been excluded from this list as he too plays a vital role.

Stable tenures are crucial to the efficient functioning of all public servants. It is, therefore, difficult to understand why assured tenures are not necessary for secretaries in charge of health, education, agriculture, rural development, for that matter, all departments.

There is an inherent connection between tenures and the selection process. The practice is that posts of joint secretary and higher are filled from among those screened and found fit for promotion. As seniority is an important criterion, the empanelment process is done batch-wise, considering all those who entered service in a given year. Again, while filling up posts, high weightage is given to the inter se seniority of those empanelled. Consequently, an officer who is on top of the approved panel would be promoted against

---

* First published in *The Hindu*, 20 October 2005.

the first available vacancy. It may so happen that the only available vacancy at a given point of time is that of additional secretary in the Ministry of Defence and the senior-most empanelled officer appointed to this post has no earlier experience of working in the security arena. The system would not consider another empanelled officer who has earlier served as director or joint secretary in the home or defence ministries merely because he or she may happen to be number seven or ten in the approved panel. Thus, briefly, all the empanelled officers are promoted against vacancies, as and when, and where, they arise.

The seniority-oriented policy virtually ensures a systemic mismatch. Adherence to seniority in promoting eligible officers to arising secretary-level vacancies generates varied difficulties. For example, an outstanding additional secretary who is senior-most on the panel and most of whose past experience has been in industry and finance may be appointed home secretary even though he or she has no more than a few months left to retire.

This situation cannot help the functioning of the security management apparatus. Provision of secured tenures will yield value only if the officers appointed to man senior posts in the security-related arena are selected from among those who have been methodically groomed for such jobs. And such grooming would be possible only if the process commences early enough, around the mid-career of officers belonging to the various feeder cadres. They have to be systematically identified and then consciously deployed in the security management arena. This would involve a total restructuring of the existing personnel management policies and procedures.

Till the required fundamental changes can be brought about, it would be profitable to seriously consider replacing 'seniority-cum-merit' with 'in depth' selections. If this is acceptable, the following would be worth considering: (i) two to three successive batches could be screened together, the screening criteria tightened and the best officers empanelled for promotion; (ii) once merit is established, an officer most suited for filling up a vacancy in the security establishment may be selected without his or her inter se seniority coming in the way. Thus, in a combined panel of two or more batches, an officer with the appropriate background could be picked for filling a vacancy that matches his or her experience. This also ensures against individual officers choosing their postings, as happens on many occasions.

To secure a meaningful outcome, it is necessary to provide continuity of tenure in the entire hierarchy of the security establishment. Management of national security concerns is no longer confined to the defence and home ministries and the Central intelligence agencies. Today, it involves virtually every department at the Centre and the corresponding agencies in the states. It would thus be naive to presume that the Central authorities would, operating on their own, be able to effectively manage national security problems. The Central apparatus requires to be fully and effectively supported by all echelons concerned in the country, particularly the police and intelligence organizations in the states. Thus it is vital to ensure that all security-related organizations in the states are also manned and directed by officials who are allowed undisturbed tenures.

The complex problems of national security management have been reviewed and analysed many times. Stressing the importance of effective national security management, it was recommended (Report of the Task Force on Internal Security, Government of India, 2000) that the government should examine the establishment of a dedicated security administration pool or cadre early. This would have talented officers from the all-India and Central services and all related professional areas (the armed forces, the Defence Research and Development Organization [DRDO], science and technology, information and broadcasting, telecommunications and the media). It was proposed that officers comprising such a pool could be deployed in the various departments and agencies responsible for security management. Subject to good performance, they could be granted open-ended tenures to enable them to acquire the much-needed expertise. This would equip them to effectively discharge their responsibilities and serve their entire careers in one or the other wing of the security establishment.

GoM DECISION

The above recommendation was considered by a group of ministers (GoM) that comprised the home minister (chairman), the defence, finance and external affairs ministers, and the national security adviser. The GoM resolved that the Department of Personnel should evolve a scheme for the establishment of a pool of officers, drawn from all services, for manning posts at all levels in the security administration apparatus. The GoM also recorded that as jobs in the security arena are relatively more demanding and correspondingly less sought after, the officers comprising the dedicated security administration pool could be compensated with suitable non-monetary incentives. The GoM's recommendations were approved by the government in early 2001. Many years have since elapsed and nothing further has been heard. Such grave delays remain unquestioned because all security-related issues are classified 'secret', even those relating to personnel management!

The security threats the country faces will not get resolved merely by granting extensions in service to a few officers in the Central apparatus. It is necessary to review and refurbish each and every element of the entire security apparatus across the various wings of the Central government and in the states. Such an exercise will succeed only if, over the next few years, all posts in the security management arena are manned by selected officers, both at the Centre and in the states, from a pool of competent personnel trained and fully equipped to discharge their duties. Finally, even such an approach will have no meaning unless it enables the pool officers to rise to the highest echelons in the states and at the Centre.

If effective security management is truly a serious concern the prime minister must convene a special meeting of the Cabinet Committee on Security to discuss the issues involved and prescribe a clear-cut policy for time-bound execution.

12

Towards a Better Understanding[*]

India's defence services (comprising the army, navy and air force) carry the high responsibility of ensuring the country's territorial integrity. Besides defending our frontiers, the services have been rendering invaluable assistance to the states in rescue and relief operations in the wake of floods, cyclones, earthquakes or any kind of disaster. The army has its statutory obligation to provide assistance to the civil authority in tackling major law and order problems, whenever the state government concerned finds itself unable to handle a serious situation on its own.

In the past such assistance was called for on rare occasions. However, over the years, with the decline in the capacity and even willingness of the state governments to deal with their emerging problems, the army's involvement has increased significantly. Further, with the emergence of insurgency in several parts of the country, the army has had to be deployed for extended periods to tackle the activities of subversive groups, some of whom have been receiving encouragement, training, weapons and financial support from Pakistan's ISI to create chaos and destabilize the established authority.

The army remained deployed in Punjab for nearly a decade in the wake of Operation Blue Star and provided crucial support in

---

[*] First published in *Deccan Herald*, 10 January 1999.

restoring normalcy. Since 1990 large elements of the army have been dealing with the serious situation created in J&K by the sustained ingress of trained militants from across the border. The army also continues to be responsible for dealing with the near-endemic insurgency in several states in the Northeast. Thus, today, the Indian army is responsible not only for guarding our frontiers but also for assisting the states in putting down insurgency. Consequently, it has emerged as a crucial factor in defending the country against external aggression and in maintaining national unity.

Under the Constitution, our military is apolitical and works under the control of the civilian authority. In the states, there is a long-established mechanism of maintaining sound relations with the army through civil–military liaison conferences, which are held annually or more often, as per requirement. These are hosted by the nearest army commander (i.e., the GOC-in-C [General Officer Commanding-in-Chief] in whose jurisdiction a state falls) and the state government by rotation. Such conferences are attended by the state chief and home secretaries and the director general of police and home guards and all senior functionaries who may be concerned with the matters listed for discussion.

These meetings provide a useful opportunity for the senior-most state functionaries to meet the army commander and his senior officers and resolve all matters of mutual interest. During service in Punjab, I had the opportunity of attending such meetings for many years and found that they provided an excellent opportunity for both sides to forge a cordial understanding which, whenever the state faced any serious situation, proved invaluable.

Each service, headed by its chief, operates through its service headquarters for the command and control of the personnel comprising its ranks. The service headquarters have their own hierarchical set-up. Below the chief are the vice chief and deputy chief (two in the army) and a number of principal staff officers (PSOs) who oversee major areas of responsibility. Each PSO is of a lieutenant general or equivalent rank.

Under the Constitution, the Union is responsible for the defence of India and for the naval, military and air forces. Under the allocation of business rules of the Government of India (1964), this responsibility is entrusted to the Ministry of Defence (MoD). The MoD, headed by the defence minister, discharges its business as per the Transaction of Business Rules of the Government of India (1964). The defence secretary is responsible for the efficient functioning of the defence department (which deals with matters relating to the three services) and is also the coordinating secretary of the MoD. The interface between each service headquarters and the MoD is extensive.

A few years ago, the government decided to remove the naval chief. There has been a spate of comments and reaction in the wake of this decision. Rather than react to all of them, I shall focus on a few aspects which caused serious damage to the image of the services and created altogether unfounded doubts and suspicions about the civil–military relationship.

It has been said that the MoD has no authority to question the chief's recommendation about the filling up of a given vacancy at senior level and that, inter alia, the naval episode resulted from the obduracy and misrepresentation of facts by the defence secretary and the MoD bureaucracy. And so it was argued that the chiefs should be liberated from the stranglehold of the MoD civilians and enabled to deal directly with the defence minister and the prime minister.

Unfortunately, this debate was clouded by issues relating to the government's decision to approve the appointment to the post of deputy chief of naval staff (DCNS) of a vice admiral who had gone to court, made allegations against the navy chief and his wife, and sought judicial intervention to be appointed DCNS. The navy chief had made counter-allegations against his vice admiral and also charged that the defence secretary colluded with the vice admiral and, further, that the MoD had been working against the interests of the services. The court rejected the petition and the government proceeded to clear the appointment of this vice admiral as DCNS.

The chief took the position that this order was 'unimplementable'. The government removed the chief, observing that its decision resulted from his continuing defiance and other acts of omission and commission.

The functioning of the services is founded on unquestioned loyalty, strict enforcement of discipline and centuries-old traditions and codes of honour. I have spent a major portion of my service career working alongside and for the services. It is most unfortunate that, following the navy chief episode, the debate has become open-ended and many statements were made which questioned the very foundations of, and ruptured, civil–military relations. Having worked in the MoD for many years, let me say that our defence services are among the best in the world. They are altogether apolitical and have continued to render dedicated service to the nation even though deployed in the most inhospitable environments. It is, therefore, of vital importance that nothing should be said or done which creates even the remotest doubt about the affection and esteem which the people of our country have for the men in uniform.

The time has come to consider past experience, reckon with existing and emerging challenges, review and appropriately revise the existing channels, procedures and decision-making levels. Needless to say, the MoD and service headquarters would have to be entrusted with enlarged authority to incur expenditures, especially insofar as they relate to the day-to-day requirements of the services. Side by side, it would be necessary to clearly define the defence secretary's role and responsibilities. If his position is to sustain in the reorganized set-up, it would be necessary to upgrade his rank to enable meaningful interrelations with the chiefs who are not inclined to deal with a junior functionary.

The MoD apparatus must work promptly and efficiently, and adequately serve the requirements of the services. It is hoped that whatever changes are made would be finalized after mature deliberation of all relevant aspects of the civil–military relationship, which must not be allowed to weaken at any cost.

13

Civil–Military Relations: Opportunities and Challenges*

At the outset, it would be useful to have reasonable clarity about what exactly we have in mind when we use the term 'civil–military relations'. I say this because at a seminar held by a defence think tank in Delhi in early 2013, a statement was made that 'unsatisfactory civil–military relations are having an adverse impact on the functioning of the military in India'. While all those who are involved in studying military matters would understand that this statement refers to the functioning of the defence apparatus, I feel that a free use of the term 'civil and military relations' should be avoided as it has the potential of causing altogether unfounded doubts and suspicions in the minds of millions of people in India.

Our armed forces, comprising the army, navy and air force, have a strength of about fourteen lakh personnel and we have over twenty-seven lakh ex-servicemen. If the families of our serving and retired officers and men are also taken into account there are more than two crore people who enjoy the trust and affection of the people of our country. I would, therefore, stress the importance of ensuring that this very warm relationship with our men and women in uniform continues. To make sure that no unfounded misgivings are created about this important relationship, I feel

---

* USI National Security Lecture 2013, Delivered on Friday, 6 December 2013.

that our strategic analysts and commentators may, instead of using the expression 'civil–military relations', comment directly on the functioning of the defence management apparatus and say whatever they wish to say.

I shall now touch upon yet another facet of civil–military interface which relates to the duty which the army has been discharging, ever since 1947, of providing aid to the civil authority and supporting affected states in combating insurgency and terrorism. In many cases, when even the police and the CPMF together were unable to handle a given disorder, the army was called upon to provide the required support.

As a consequence, the army has continued to be deployed in several parts of the country in considerable strength, and for prolonged periods, to carry out anti-insurgency and anti-terrorism operations. On many occasions, the operations carried out by the army, in conjunction with the state and Central paramilitary forces, have led to complaints and allegations from the local population about the violation of their rights. And there has been a continuing debate, for the past several years, on whether or not the Armed Forces Special Powers Act (AFSPA) should continue to apply to the disturbed areas where the army has been carrying out sustained operations for combating insurgency and terrorism. While every uniformed force, in whichever area it is called upon to operate, is duty-bound to ensure that the people's civil rights are protected, it is equally necessary for the Centre and the affected states to collectively evolve an acceptable approach which ensures that the personnel of the military formations which are involved in carrying out counter-insurgency or anti-terrorism operations are provided the requisite legal protection.

As law and order situations continue to arise in the future, in one or the other part of the country, it would be useful, in the long term, if well-planned and time-bound steps are implemented for increasing the strength and logistical resources of the state police organizations and upgrading their professional capabilities for meeting future challenges. The development of the police into a more effective force should, hopefully, lead to a progressive reduction in the recurring need to call out the army. I would also add that the requisite training and professional upgradation of the police, as also of the CPMF, can be most usefully assisted by the army, which has well-equipped and competent training centres all over the country. In fact, internal security management would become far more effective if the army were to develop operational interoperability with the police and identified CPMF.

I now come to the question of the civil–military balance, which essentially concerns the functioning of the defence apparatus and the varied issues which may arise from the professional interface between the defence ministry and the military leadership of the three armed forces. The various elements which comprise this theme fall within the arena of higher defence management. I shall try to focus on some of the more important aspects of this theme.

A growing number of former senior officers of the armed forces have been writing on issues relating to higher defence management. These commentators broadly fall into two groups: one which largely focuses on the failings of the Ministry of Defence and the other which also speaks about the deficiencies in the internal functioning of the armed forces. I shall rapidly go over the more significant dissatisfactions voiced by both these groups.

A criticism which has been frequently raised alleges that impediments arise in the functioning of the defence ministry because the civilian officers posted in the ministry exercise authority which far exceeds their mandate. I shall examine the basis of this misperception and try to explain the true position in simple terms.

First and foremost, in any discussion on defence management, it is extremely important to bear in mind that in our democratic, parliamentary framework, the power lies with the elected representatives of the people, from among whom cabinet ministers are appointed. The ministers have the responsibility of managing the affairs of the departments under their charge and decide all important matters except those which are required to be submitted to the Cabinet, Cabinet Committee on Security, prime minister, president or other specified authorities. The civil servants working in the various departments of the Government of India are the tools or the instrumentalities for assisting the ministers in finalizing policies and then ensuring that the same are effectively executed.

The Constitution of India lays down the framework within which the Union, i.e., the Government of India and the states are required to carry out their respective responsibilities. List 1 of the Seventh Schedule of the Constitution enumerates the subjects which are to be dealt with by the Government of India. In this List, the Government of India has been, inter alia, assigned responsibility for ensuring the 'Defence of India and every part thereof'. The supreme command of the armed forces rests in the president. The responsibility for national defence vests with the Cabinet. This responsibility is discharged through the Ministry of Defence, which provides the policy framework and wherewithal to the armed forces to discharge their responsibilities in the context of the defence of the country. The defence minister is the head of the Ministry of Defence. The principal task of the defence ministry is to obtain policy directions of the government on all defence and security-related matters and see that these are implemented by the service headquarters, inter-service organizations, production establishments and research and development organizations.

As provided by the Constitution, the various subjects in List 1 are distributed among the different departments in accordance with the Government of India (Allocation of Business) Rules 1961. Under these Rules, matters relating to the defence of India have been allocated to the Ministry of Defence which comprises the department of defence, department of defence production, department of defence research and development and the department of ex-servicemen welfare.

Further, under the Government of India (Transaction of Business) Rules 1961, 'all business allotted to a department specified under the government of India (Allocation of Business) Rules 1961, shall be disposed of by, or under the general or special directions of, the minister-in-charge' of the department (Rule 3), subject to the provision of these Rules.

The Transaction of Business Rules further stipulate that 'In each department, the Secretary (which term includes the Special Secretary or Additional Secretary or Joint Secretary in independent charge) shall be the administrative head thereof, and shall be responsible for the proper transaction of business and the careful observance of these rules in that department' (Rule 11).

Thus, as per the constitutional framework, the overall responsibility for the functioning of the Ministry of Defence rests entirely on the defence minister and the responsibility for ensuring that the business of the department of defence is transacted strictly in conformity with the Government of India (Transaction of Business) Rules, 1961, is vested in the defence secretary.

From my own experience of working in the defence ministry for many years I can state, without an iota of doubt, that officers working in the defence ministry discharge their duties with great care and all important matters relating to the four departments of the defence ministry are decided by the defence minister, except those cases which are required to be submitted to other designated authorities.

The defence ministry, then, is clearly responsible to the Government of India for dealing with all matters relating to the defence of India and the armed forces of the Union and, further, as provided under the Defence Services Regulations, the chiefs of the services are responsible to the president, through the defence ministry, for the command, discipline, recruitment, training, organization, administration and preparation of war of their respective services.

The civilian face of the defence ministry is represented by the defence minister, his junior ministerial colleagues, defence secretary and the other three administrative secretaries in the ministry and, say, another 15–20 officers of joint secretary level and above in all the four departments of the ministry. During my days in the defence ministry, a dozen officers of joint secretary level in the four departments were dealing with all the matters which were received from the army, navy and air headquarters, commonly referred to as the Service Headquarters (SHQ), and from several inter-service organizations.

The arrangements which obtained in my time have undergone very significant changes after the amendment of the Government of India (Transaction of Business Rules) and the establishment of the Integrated army, navy, air force Defence Staff Headquarters of the Ministry of Defence. The Integrated Headquarters (IHQ) are involved with policy formulation in regard to the defence of India and the armed forces of the Union and are responsible for providing the executive directions required in the implementation of policies laid down by the Ministry of Defence.

A frequently voiced dissatisfaction is that the civilians who are posted in the defence ministry do not have adequate experience of working in this arena and also do not have long enough tenures to gain specialization for effectively dealing with military matters. This perception is largely true. Only a few among those who get posted in the Ministry of Defence, particularly officers at the joint secretary and equivalent level, have done previous stints in the defence or home ministries. As regards tenures: while the Central Secretariat Services officers may serve for long periods, the officers on deputation appointed to posts at the level of director and joint secretary enjoy average tenures of five years. I strongly believe that it is necessary to remedy this situation and I had made a definitive recommendation in this regard over a decade ago, about which I shall comment a little later.

Some commentators have alleged that the role of the political leaders has been hijacked by IAS officers and what obtains in the defence ministry today is 'bureaucratic control and not civilian political control of the military'. It has been further argued that the civil services have succeeded in having their own way essentially because the political leadership has little to no experience or expertise in handling defence matters, has little to no interest, and lacks the will to support reforms in the defence management apparatus. This line of thinking is carried forward to conclude that as the defence ministry does not have the confidence and capability to adjudicate on the competing claims and demands made by the individual services, each service largely follows its own course and enlarges its role as per the whims and fancies of successive chiefs.

I have already explained at some length the constitutional framework within which the defence ministry and its officers are required to function. However, to eradicate any misperceptions, it would be most useful if the curricula of the various military training institutions also contain a suitably designed course for enabling the officer cadres to gain adequate awareness of the working of the Constitution of India and, side by side, to enhance their political awareness. Doing this would also provide a useful opportunity for appointing well-qualified civilian teachers at the various military training academies with whom the trainee officers could have informal discussions on varied matters in which they may be interested.

As regards the assertion that the individual services largely take their own decisions on account of the defence ministry's failure to enforce effective control, there cannot be any debate about the crucial need for the Integrated Defence Staff to work towards securing a level of joint-ness. This will enable critical inter se prioritization of the varied demands projected by the individual services and, based thereon, evolution of a closely integrated defence plan which has a 10–15-year perspective.

I now come to the views expressed by several former senior officers who are unhappy with the internal health, morale and discipline of the services. Some of them are of the view that issues about civilian control have arisen essentially because successive defence ministers have chosen not to exercise the requisite influence and control and have been particularly amiss in never questioning the chiefs about the logic and assumptions relating to the execution of military plans, as this vital responsibility has been left entirely to the service headquarters. Operation Blue Star, Operation Brass Tacks, Exercise Checker Board, IPKF operations in Sri Lanka and several other events are cited as examples of serious avoidable failures which happened because of the lack of clarity about the goals to be achieved and on account of major gaps in the operational plans. It is asked why such failures have never been subjected to any questioning or audit, as should have been done in a well-run system. Successive generations of military officers have been denied the opportunity of learning from past mistakes because of the government's failure to allow publication of the histories of the wars in which India has been engaged since 1947.

This important issue was taken note of by the Group of Ministers on National Security (2001) and a committee to review the publication of military histories was set up by the defence minister in 2002. This committee, which I was called upon to chair, gave a clear recommendation that the histories of the 1962, 1965 and 1971 wars should be published without any further delay. This was in 2003. I gather that the history of the 1965 war has since been published.

Some commentators have taken the position that difficulties arise in the functioning of the defence ministry because defence ministers do not have past exposure to military matters. This is not a well-founded notion. The USA and various European countries faced two prolonged world wars and two to three generations of their youth were compelled to undergo conscriptions. Consequently, for many years in the post-World War periods, a number of ministers in these countries had earlier served in the armed forces and had been directly exposed to military functioning. Today, however, even in these countries there aren't many elected persons with earlier exposure to serving in the military. In India, we have never had any conscription. Recruitments to all our forces are done on a voluntary basis. It would not be logical, therefore, to suggest that our defence ministers should necessarily have been exposed to military matters.

It is also disturbing to hear angry statements that the defence ministry has not been devoting timely attention to dealing with its tasks. During my days in the defence ministry, I worked with eight defence ministers, of whom five were the prime ministers of the country, and can say, without any hesitation whatsoever, that even the prime ministers who held charge of defence ministry remained most seriously concerned about issues regarding national security management despite being burdened with a horde of crisis situations on varied fronts. However, a factor which invariably came in the way of prompt and satisfactory resolution, such as may have been possible in those troubled times, was our failure to present to the defence minister clear-cut options based on advice received from the Chiefs of Staff Committee.

Here, it is relevant to recall the practice that the chiefs raise no significant matter in the defence minister's Monday morning meetings and seek to discuss substantive issues only in one-on-one meetings with him and, if possible, also with the prime minister. I also recall that whenever the chiefs met the defence minister together and presented him with even a broadly agreed approach, there was no delay in decisions being promptly arrived at and speedily promulgated. While, after the establishment of the Integrated Defence Staff, the decision-making processes have hopefully, improved very significantly, I would reiterate the importance of ensuring that the defence ministry functions on the basis of dynamic coordination between the civilian and military elements. I would also stress that integrated approaches can materialize if decision making is based on processes which are rooted in joint-ness.

My memory goes back to the late 1980s when the defence ministry's functioning was, among other factors, most adversely affected by a severe financial crisis in the country. Recognizing the understandable worries and tensions within the defence ministry, Prime Minister V.P. Singh, who was also the defence minister at that time, set up a Committee on Defence Expenditure (CDE), which was charged to review the existing defence set-up and recommend practical solutions to rationalize military expenditures. I was the defence secretary at that time. Arun Singh, who was chairman of this committee, consulted me informally about the recommendations evolved by his group and I gave him my personal opinion that while the proposal to create a joint chiefs of staff (JCS) set-up for advising the defence minister on all military matters would necessarily have to be processed at the political level, there could be no difficulty whatsoever in implementing all the other recommendations for enforcing economies, closing redundant ordnance factories, rationalizing the functioning of the finance wing and enlarging the existing administrative and financial delegations. The Chiefs of Staff Committee (COSC), after examining the CDE report, communicated that none of the committee's recommendations would be accepted if the government did not accept the recommended restructuring of the Chiefs of Staff Committee. To secure better resource management, the defence ministry went ahead and ordered financial delegations up to the army command and equivalent levels, placed an internal financial adviser (IFA) in each service headquarters and directed several other useful changes.

The process of defence reforms did not move much further till May 1998 when the successful underground nuclear tests at Pokhran catapulted India into the exclusive league of nuclear power states. Needless to say, this sudden development cast very high responsibility on the Government of India, particularly on the defence ministry. This led to the establishment of various arrangements and structures for handling strategic issues and decisions. Thus, the National Security Council was set up in November 1998 and a National Security Adviser (NSA) was appointed at about the same time.

Then, in the summer of 1999 came the Kargil war, which took the country entirely by surprise and generated grave misgivings about the defence apparatus and serious concerns about the army's preparedness. The Kargil Review Committee (KRC) was set up to undertake a thorough review of the events leading up to the Pakistani aggression in the Kargil district and to recommend measures for safeguarding national security against such armed intrusions. The KRC report (2000) was speedily examined by a group of ministers (GoM) which was chaired by Home Minister L.K. Advani. For undertaking national security reforms the GoM set up four task forces, one of which was on higher defence management.

Among the foremost recommendations made by this task force was the creation of the Chief of Defence Staff (CDS) who, supported by the Vice Chief of Defence Staff, would head the Integrated Defence Staff to improve the planning process, promote 'joint-ness' among the armed forces and provide single-point military advice to the government. While the group of ministers endorsed almost all the major recommendations of the task force on higher defence management, the proposal regarding the creation of a Chief of Defence Staff suffered from the lack of collective support by the three services and failed to secure approval for want of political consensus.

I shall now briefly mention certain issues which continue to affect the efficient functioning of the defence apparatus:

• While some improvements have been achieved in the past years, the defence ministry must enforce strict measures to ensure that the ordnance factories, defence PSUs, DRDO establishments and other agencies concerned function efficiently to deliver supplies and services as per the envisaged time and cost schedules; prolonged delays cause serious difficulties for the armed forces and large economic losses, as the lack of certainty about supplies from indigenous sources compels expensive imports whenever any emergency arises.

- While there have been notable advances in the rationalization of procurement policies and procedures, there is still a need to ensure speedy acquisition proceedings as delays altogether nullify the 'make or buy' approach.
- While the individual services enjoy the autonomy of making their own selection of weapons, equipment and systems, the Integrated Services Headquarters must take effective steps to establish a tri-service approach in regard to such decisions – doing so will engender very significant financial savings.
- The defence planning process has still to get established; the tenth and eleventh defence plans were implemented without receiving formal approvals and while the long term integrated perspective plan (LTIPP) has since been finalized, it is still viewed as a totalling up of the wish lists of the individual services; the Integrated Defence Staff must devote urgent attention towards finalizing a fully integrated defence plan with at least a 10–15 year perspective.
- The services enjoy the authority of virtually settling their own manpower policies; the pro rata percentage representation of arms and services in the army needs to be modified forthwith as it is virtually a 'quota system' which breeds group loyalties and cuts at the very roots of joint-ness within the service.
- But above all, there must be no further delay in finalizing the National Security Doctrine, on the basis of which integrated threat assessments could be made.

Over the years, efforts have been made by the defence ministry to promote joint-ness through the integration of planning, training and other systems so that, progressively, a tri-service approach could get fully established. Thus, in the 1980s, two very important steps were taken: the establishment of the Army Training Command (ARTRAC) and the Directorate General of Defence Planning Staff (DGDPS). It would be profitable, even at this stage, if the Chiefs of Staff Committee were to set up an expert group to review the functioning so far of these two institutions and identify the reasons why both these crucial organizations could not achieve their objectives which were, inter alia, envisaged to promote the establishment of joint-ness and a tri-service approach.

While the functioning of the defence apparatus has been getting steadily refined, I feel that the continuing lack of consensus among the three services is thwarting the achievement of the vital objective of joint-ness. A number of joint service institutions have come into existence in the post-Kargil period. Among the new institutions, frequent references are made to the Integrated Defence Staff (IDS), Defence Intelligence Agency (DIA), Andaman and Nicobar Command and the Strategic Forces Command. While it may be far too early to rejoice over these recently established inter-agency institutions, it is disconcerting to learn that the individual services are not doing all that is required to see that these new organizations get fully established without facing delays and difficulties. A former army chief is quoted to say that the Integrated Defence Staff is 'a redundancy in military bureaucracy'; the founder director of the Defence Intelligence Agency is quoted to bring out that 'the Defence Intelligence Agency cannot deliver as the intelligence agencies of the three services feel threatened by it'; and about the Integrated Defence Staff it is stated that 'the Services will never allow this body to function as they feel threatened that it will start examining the basis of their budgetary proposals, acquisition plans and force structures'.

The time has come for the individual services to close ranks and get collectively concerned about the major threats and formidable challenges which we face in our close neighbourhood and beyond. The global security environment is continuing to become growingly complex and huge uncertainties loom large on various fronts.

Our military has also to be concerned about the consequences of the economic meltdown and the strong likelihood of the allocations for defence facing a significant decline in the coming years. To prepare to successfully meet future challenges, it is of the highest importance that the individual services shed all reservations and establish meaningful joint-ness. The pursuit of a truly tri-service approach will not only reduce functional overlaps but also contribute towards reducing wasteful duplications and redundancies. I learn that the Integrated Defence Staff have already promulgated a joint doctrine on the Indian armed forces, which is presently undergoing revision because of the differing views of the service headquarters on several important issues. Therefore, I would reiterate the crucial importance of ensuring the urgent finalization of the joint doctrine which covers all aspects of integrated operations. Any delay in this regard would come in the way of the armed forces preparing themselves fully for delivering an effective response when any emergency arises in the future.

In view of the serious economic problems being faced the world over, many countries are exploring various approaches for containing and restricting the large expenditures being incurred on maintaining their armed forces. Our defence ministry must keep a very close watch on the rising cost of maintaining the military apparatus and ensuring that the high cost of the longer-term acquisitions can be met from within the future availability of resources. Side by side, urgent attention needs to be paid to reducing dependency on continuing imports of weapons and systems. This would require a very vigorous revving up of the ongoing indigenization programmes, and DRDO and defence production units joining hands with the private sector to yield speedier results. In the past, only the navy has initiated systematic steps to foster indigenization of their major platforms and systems and deserve all praise for the wonderful outcomes which they have already been able to achieve.

India is not the only country which is engaged in dealing with problems which relate to the functioning of the defence management apparatus. Many democracies have been facing such problems and, benefitting from their own experiences, several important countries have established strong parliamentary oversight bodies to monitor all the important issues relating to the functioning of their armed forces. Some countries have even inducted external experts to monitor their ongoing defence reform processes.

India cannot and must not be left behind in doing all that needs to be done for strengthening and enhancing our national security interests. I have long been of the view that we need to develop our own model of defence management, which vigorously promotes and sustains military professionalism while being fully in tune with our constitutional framework and in harmony with our glorious traditions of soldiering. The model to be evolved should also not be excessively encumbered with hierarchical fixations which are rooted in our colonial past.

On the basis of my own experience, I would say that it would be an ideal situation if the service chiefs were to collaborate closely and for the Chiefs of Staff Committee to take the required decisions to pave the way for the future and establish joint-ness, brick by brick. In the past few decades many useful opportunities were lost because of the lack of convergence in the views of the service headquarters.

If joint-ness and a tri-service approach cannot be achieved soon enough, perhaps the only option left may be to proceed towards replacing the existing single-service Acts by an Armed Forces Act which would lay a statutory basis for achieving joint-ness and delineating the roles, duties and missions of the armed forces, as also the procedures and modalities relating to the functioning of the defence apparatus. Here, it may not be out of place to recall that the USA achieved its objectives by promulgating the Goldwater Nichols Act in 1986, after nearly four decades of experimentation under the aegis of its National Security Act. And more recently, because of the serious budgetary problems faced by the country, the UK has been devoting high-level attention to introducing reforms in its defence management apparatus. The Levene Report has sought to clarify the respective roles and responsibilities of ministers, civilian officers and the military at the policy, strategic and operational levels.

Insofar as the tenures of civilians working in the Ministry of Defence are concerned, it is necessary to post officers who have been adequately trained for working in the security administration arena and, if their performance is satisfactory, allowed to continue for extended periods. It is also necessary to take suitable steps to reduce the rather worrying differences in the perceptions of civil and military officers about their respective roles.

In this context, I was asked in 2001 to chair a task force to work out the curricula for organizing a continuing joint civil and military training programme on national security which would be undergone by brigadiers and major generals and officers of equivalent rank from the three defence services, IAS, IPS, IFS and central paramilitary forces. As the training settled down, participants would also be drawn from the media, industry and other arenas. On the basis of my recommendations, the first two-week Joint Civil and Military Training Programme on National Security commenced at the IAS Training Academy at Mussoorie in February 2003. This programme has been successfully continuing for over a decade now and the twentieth course commenced at Mussoorie in November 2013. It would be beneficial if the defence ministry were to review this programme and suitably recast its contents to meet the existing and emerging scenarios.

Recurring media reports in the recent past about controversial interviews relating to personnel issues, the defence minister's decision being challenged in the apex court, and several other unseemly scandals have marred the army's glorious image and dragged the services into the cesspool of partisan and parochial politics. This has caused divisiveness and serious damage to the very fabric of our military. It is unfortunate that any questioning of deviations from well-established norms is viewed as questioning the very loyalty of the entire Indian Army. Such incidents, which have a grave adverse effect on the morale of the armed forces, must not be allowed to recur under any circumstances. The time has perhaps come to review the entire existing basis of promotions and appointments to the higher echelons in the three services.

The patriotism and professionalism of the men and women of our armed forces is second to none among militaries the world over. Our fearless military personnel, who maintain an eternal vigil on our land, sea and air frontiers, have successfully thwarted successive aggressions and safeguarded the territorial integrity and sovereignty of our motherland, laying down their lives for the country.

I have a very long association of working with the military. For the past several years I have been serving in Jammu and Kashmir where I have had the opportunity of observing from very close quarters the extremely difficult circumstances in which the men and women of our army operate round the year, in severe weather and harsh terrains. I pay my humble tribute to our valiant soldiers and reiterate that there should be no doubt ever, of any kind, about the devotion and loyalty of our military. Let nothing be ever said or done which generates any kind of debate or controversy which mars the glorious image or affects the morale of the fourteen lakh officers and men of our armed forces.

Our national security concerns demand that all interests and all institutions of national power are brought to work closely together to further the country's interest and build a militarily and economically strong India which enjoys the trust and respect of all our neighbours. In conclusion I would say to all my friends in uniform and to all my civilian colleagues: the country must come first, always and ever, for 'who lives if India dies'?

Governance

Challenges and Opportunities

14

National Governance since Independence[*]

During their rule, the British demarcated the political geography of the country entirely on the basis of their colonial interests and administrative convenience. As the annexation of territories progressed, provinces and directly administered units were carved out in utter disregard of the culture, religion, affinities and aspirations of the people. Some of the provinces were several times larger in area and population than countries in Europe. The primary focus was on the fullest exploitation of the country's resources and, except to the extent necessary to subserve the interests of the Crown, no attention was paid to human or economic development. However, notwithstanding the vast array of adversities and humiliations to which the 'natives' were subjected, British rule engendered one significant development – India's large and heterogeneous population was controlled through a countrywide administrative apparatus, from the village upwards, which was effectively directed by a strong Central authority, a phenomenon unknown in the pre-British period.

The administration of British India was effectively managed by the Indian Civil Service (ICS) officers who held all the vital

* First published in V.A. Pai Panandiker (ed.), *Fifty Years of Swaraj – Highlights and Shadows*, New Delhi: Konarak Publishers, 1998.

('strategic' as the British called them) posts in the provinces and at the Centre. ICS officers, appointed by the secretary of state in England, enjoyed high privileges and protected tenures. They were authoritarian, all-powerful, and were, for good reason, described as the 'steel frame' of the empire.

In the prolonged period of struggle for the attainment of freedom, the Indian National Congress was able to develop its cadres from the ground level upwards. Thus, when the British, under increasing pressure, decided to grant provincial autonomy (under the Government of India Act, 1935) the governors were replaced by the newly elected premiers and their councils of ministers who became responsible for the administration of the transferred subjects. Many ICS officers who did not find it compatible to serve under the elected representatives of the people sought retirement and left the country. In the succeeding decade, the Congress was able to gain useful experience in parliamentary democracy and managing the business of government.

Consequently, when the transfer of power took place in 1947, the assumption of authority by the national leadership did not pose any problem. The structures of civil, police and judicial administration were taken over and run by the ICS and Indian Police (IP) officers, supported by officers of the provincial civil services. The sudden departure of British and Muslim officials had seriously dislocated the functioning of the administration. This gap was partly filled by the induction of suitably qualified officers from the army. The takeover of the three defence services – army, navy and air force – did not pose any insurmountable problems.

The newly established governments at the Centre and in the provinces faced serious and pressing problems. The period leading up to 15 August 1947 had witnessed Hindu–Muslim communal confrontations on a massive scale, especially in Bengal, Punjab, Sindh and the NWFP, and the massacre of lakhs of families whose properties were looted and burnt. This had led to the large-scale migration of people from both the communities to safer areas.

Later, the announcement of the territories which would comprise Pakistan led to the inflow to India of millions of refugees from East and West Pakistan. They had to be provided food, shelter, clothing, medical care and, soon enough, means of resettlement.

There were serious problems on other fronts: the continuing communal violence had to be contained and public order restored; the restive elements demanding independence – Nagas in the Northeast and Akalis in Punjab – had to be dealt with; acute shortages of foodgrains and other essential items had to be met and 550 princely states had to be integrated within the Indian Union. As if these were not enough, the government had to deal with the invasion of the Kashmir Valley organized by Pakistan in the winter of 1947.

The government was successful in managing the situation. This was possible as Jawaharlal Nehru's Cabinet comprised highly educated, experienced and outstanding personalities of reputed integrity who were capable of providing mature guidance and effective direction to the bureaucracy. On 26 January 1950, the Constitution was adopted and India emerged as a sovereign, democratic republic. The first parliamentary elections were held and Nehru continued as the prime minister.

The Constitution of India seeks to promote the welfare of the people by securing and promoting a social order in which justice – social, economic and political – shall inform the functioning of all public institutions. Being seriously concerned with the communal tensions and violence which had been unleashed during 1946–47, the founding fathers of the Constitution devised a federal framework of governance and wisely provided for a strong Centre which would be able to curb and contain divisive trends and safeguard national integrity. To meet situations of serious public disorder or the failure of states to govern by the rule of law, the Constitution provides for direct Central control, through imposition of president's rule.

If honestly and efficiently operated by the states and the Centre, the framework of governance ingrained in the Constitution contains adequate provisions for the achievement of national integration and securing the envisioned goals of a welfare state. The state is expected to take all necessary measures to achieve the objective of social welfare and a just economic system and to provide compulsory free education, public health, etc. The Fundamental Rights prohibit the practice of untouchability and no citizen can be discriminated against on the grounds of sex, place of birth, caste or religion. Reservation is provided for the Scheduled Castes and Tribes, to enable them to join the mainstream.

Nehru served as India's prime minister for the first seventeen years (1947–64). Imbued with high values, a truly secular temperament and a deep commitment to establishing a socialistic pattern of society, he attached great importance to public institutions and administrative structures being run honestly and efficiently. He abhorred religious bigotry, by whomsoever practised, and repeatedly voiced his concern that its encouragement in any form would endanger the very unity of the country. His vision of inculcating the spirit of nationalism in every aspect of life fired him with untiring zeal to bring India into a single framework of thought and action in which 'every man, woman and child has a fair deal and attains a minimum standard of living'. Despite the fact that other great leaders of the time – Vallabhbhai Patel, Abul Kalam Azad, J.B. Kripalani, Purushottam Das Tandon, Jayaprakash Narayan and others – did not share and support all of Nehru's approaches, his vision and deep commitment strongly influenced the governance of India during the formative years.

As observed earlier, the country faced enormous problems after the attainment of Independence. In the face of a large and growing population, illiteracy and large-scale poverty, the state had to play a key role in securing rapid economic growth. Without going into excessive detail regarding the Nehru–Patel disagreements in the Constituent Assembly on their respective approaches to nation building (Patel favoured a larger role for the private sector while Nehru was devoted to establishing a strong public sector) it may be re-emphasized that our Constitution, both through its specific prescriptions and the Directive Principles, provides an excellent framework of institutions and mechanisms for the salutary governance of the country and the achievement of balanced human and economic growth to forge a strong and vibrant nation.

Vallabhbhai Patel, independent India's first home minister, was of the considered view that if the country was to be held together, law and order maintained and timely results achieved in tackling the tasks of nation building, it would be necessary to retain the scheme of all-India services. Thus, the ICS and Indian Police (IP) were succeeded by the Indian Administrative Service (IAS) and the Indian Police Service (IPS), both constituted under an Act of parliament. Selected on the basis of an all-India competitive examination, IAS and IPS officers would comprise the best available talent to man the pivotal posts in the states and at the Centre.

Today the Central government apparatus is run by officers of the three all-India Services (IAS, IPS, IFoS) and about two dozen Central services. Except for the Foreign Office, which has a stand-alone set-up managed by officers of the Indian Foreign Service (IFS), every department/ministry in the government of India is administered by a secretary to the government belonging to the IAS or any of the specialized services like posts, railways, water resources, telecommunications, atomic energy, science and technology, defence science research, oceanography, medical research, etc. The cabinet secretary is the head of all the civil services and reports to the prime minister, who is at the apex of the administrative structure at the Centre.

The entire administrative machinery in the states and at the Centre functions within the ambit of the Transaction of Business Rules which flow from the Constitution. Adherence to these rules and the standing orders promulgated thereunder (these orders, issued by the secretary with the approval of the minister, cover all aspects relating to the arrangement and disposal of work in the department) is envisaged to lay down the levels of responsibility in the functioning of every department and, consequently, the accountability of its functionaries, all of whom work under the overall direction and control of the minister-in-charge of the department/ministry.

Allocated to state cadres, AIS officers would gain useful experience of working in the districts and later, on deputation to the Centre, provide valuable inputs on the ground realities for evolving sound and relevant nationwide development programmes and policies. Working at the Centre, they would develop a wider vision and national perspective which, on repatriation to their parent cadres, would strengthen their functioning in the states.

As the IAS and IPS cadres would be managed by the Centre, it was envisaged that, while working in the states, they would be unafraid to render objective advice and carry out their tasks without fear of political interference or influence. Patel was also of the view that the all-India services would act as a unifying factor and contribute to promoting strong and meaningful Centre–state relations.

Another strategy for securing cohesion and integration, consistently pursued by Nehru throughout his helmsmanship of the country, was to lay the foundations of a just and equitable economy. This led to the adoption of the centralized planning model in which the public sector would play an important role. The Planning Commission, set up in 1950, was to concern itself with virtually every aspect of human and economic development; the five-year Plans would generate balanced growth and reduction of inequalities. In recent years, the state-led planning approach has been criticized and held responsible for failures on many fronts. But we have to remember that the British bequeathed to us a backward and feudal agrarian structure, an impoverished industrial sector and, overall, an economy which had no potential whatever for resource mobilization and investment.

Even though the various development schemes and programmes contained in the successive five-year plans were not implemented with the required commitment and equal efficiency in all the states, the country achieved significant results in regard to the abolition of zamindari, reduction of inequalities in the rural economy through the imposition of ceilings on the size of land holdings, allotment of surplus lands to the landless farmers, protection of the rights of tenants, establishment of cooperative credit and service societies throughout the country to support the small farmers, and other measures.

The establishment of multipurpose dam projects and fertilizer production units contributed vitally to the success, in subsequent years, of the Green Revolution and the most outstanding achievement of self-sufficiency in the production of foodgrains. Attention was devoted to the production of steel, cement, coal, power, atomic energy, and establishing capacity for the manufacture of heavy machinery, locomotives, ships and aircraft. The railway network was expanded, and roads, bridges and highways were developed to extend and improve communications all over the country. Programmes were launched to enhance facilities for the provision of education, public health, drinking water and housing. Side by side, after the humiliation faced in the 1962 conflict with China, the development of indigenous capacities for defence production also received attention.

The centralized planning process, coupled with the planning mechanisms set up in the states, contributed significantly to the development of agriculture and industry and related infrastructure. The establishment of a nationwide chain of scientific and industrial research organizations, alongside the growth of medical, engineering, agricultural and technical institutions and universities, generated a steady stream of scientific and technically qualified manpower which, in subsequent years, enabled the absorption of advanced technologies and the success of modernization plans.

Looking back, despite failings on several fronts, the first two decades (1947–67) were, on the whole, a period of steady and purposeful growth. Also, the country held together and successfully negated three attempts by Pakistan to violate our sovereignty, in 1947, 1965 and 1971. The 1962 Sino–Indian debacle, perhaps not merely a military failure, also had a positive effect: it enhanced our national security perceptions and compelled our defence structures towards better preparedness.

I will not go into a detailed account of the failures of governance in the past fifty years. Whatever be the classical or present-day definitions of governance (today, references are made to 'good' governance to signify that what is being delivered is 'poor'), it is no longer possible to ignore the common man's perception of how the country is being run. The man on the street does not understand political philosophies or matters of high policy and has, therefore, little concern for them. Thus, while governance and government are not synonymous, what has become increasingly important is the net outcome of the day-to-day governmental functioning in the states, especially in those elements which concern the welfare of the average citizen.

Today, we are in the midst of serious failures and grave dangers on many fronts. We have not been able to check the growth of population, which has increased almost three times in size since 1947. The high rate of our population increase has the effect of negating whatever gains are secured on the developmental side. The gap between the increasing demand for essential items of consumption and the actual supply thereof has inescapably led to problems and tensions. The unabated population growth; failure of the states to secure people's participation in community development and to execute developmental schemes and programmes within the planned cost and time frames; brazen misuse and embezzlement of scarce resources specially allocated for implementing programmes to uplift the poor and neglected segments of our society, inefficiency and corruption in the administrative cadres, and other serious aberrations have resulted in the failure of state governments to achieve the avowed welfare goals and reduce poverty. While there are varying estimates of those who subsist below the poverty line, virtually one-third of our population is clearly poverty-stricken.

The failures in successfully implementing measures to stabilize the population growth and reducing poverty can be directly related to the failure in achieving the goal of universal literacy. Half of our population is still illiterate. The states have not shown the requisite political commitment to implement literacy and educational programmes. In Kerala, which succeeded in doing so, the rates of population growth and maternal and infant mortality are the lowest in the country, comparable to those which obtain in the developed countries. This has, in turn, led to improved health and enhanced potential for higher productivity. The other signal failure relates to the progressive spread of dishonesty, corruption and irregularities in governmental functioning in the states. The protection of corrupt elements by the elected executive has, over the years, resulted in ruining the functioning of vital public institutions and perversion of policies, systems and procedures. The resulting situation has most adversely affected the interests of the common man, with consequential distrust and cynicism about the very role of government.

Corruption in public life, not unknown elsewhere in the world, can perhaps be contained by enforcing legal, administrative and other measures. However, it has an altogether different connotation when it penetrates day-to-day administration and affects the welfare of the common man. Unfortunately, this has happened in our country. Ministers and chief ministers in the states have been exploiting their authority to extort 'contributions' and 'donations' allegedly to augment their party funds for contesting elections to various bodies in the democratic structure. Fund gathering has assumed the scale of organized business and has affected the functioning of governmental organizations and has, over time, led to the replacement of the rule of law with patronage, nepotism and corruption. Officials who resist unlawful and irregular directions are labelled 'unsuitable' and eased out to peripheral or non-jobs and even harassed and humiliated with rigged-up complaints of dishonesty. Honest and upright officers are transferred from place to place or kept without jobs till they 'mend' their ways. Side by side, pliant and dishonest functionaries have emerged as trusted lieutenants and, irrespective of their seniority and competence, assigned to head organizations with large budgets or those which involve dealings with business and industry. Such officers, given out-of-turn promotions and other visible favours, have emerged as members of politico-administrative coteries which run the states.

The growing corruption of the appointed executive has, over the years, had the most damaging effect on the functioning of public institutions and administrative structures. The direct linkages between chief ministers and ministers with their 'trusted' officers in the districts and in the state secretariats have resulted in vitiating the well-established channels of command and control. This has, in turn, led to indiscipline and loss of accountability, generating inefficiency and brazen insensitivity to the problems of the poor and the needy. In the past, officers were required to strictly adhere to clearly laid down channels of communication and contact with their superiors for the redress of their personal problems or official grievances. Besides, they were afraid of acquiring a reputation for approaching political elements to advance their career interests. Also, the large majority of entrants to public services could not easily deviate from the established norms of service conduct for fear of an adverse reaction from their peer groups. Another factor which strongly influenced young officers was the impeccable public image of their superiors who served as role models.

This has been systematically shattered by the political executive which, compelled by their limited and self-serving objectives, has been giving preference to 'committed' officers who unquestioningly carry out its unlawful behests. Thus, over the years, the highest appointments in the state governments – the chief secretary (CS) and the director general of police (DGP) – need not be held by the senior-most officers of proven competence and known integrity but by pliant elements, some of whom may even be facing inquiries or were questioned in the past. This has resulted in the best available officers being sidelined and discarded. Having positioned their 'own men' as heads of the civil, police and other services and at vantage points in the field, the chief ministers are no longer concerned about the health of the administrative machinery, and much less about complying with the well-established norms in regard to the posting, transfer and promotion of officers of the various cadres.

Consequently, a situation has arisen, as in Uttar Pradesh for the past several years, of hundreds of field and secretariat officers being transferred every month. This is done in utter disregard of the tenure policies and the brief periods for which the officers may have actually served on their last assignments. This has not left IAS and IPS officers unscathed. District magistrates (DMs) and superintendents of police (SPs) and secretariat officers of various levels are shifted within days of taking over their new assignments. Besides the harassment caused to those repeatedly being transferred, such shifts have an adverse effect on the maintenance of law and order and implementation of crucial developmental and poverty alleviation programmes. Another most disturbing aspect of this 'transfer industry', run under the direct control of the state chief ministers, is the open public talk that a price is placed on every post and large sums are collected from those who make successful bids!

Such exploitation has resulted in cynicism and loss of morale among the state bureaucracies. The CSs and DGPs seek to protect their reputations by claiming that the transfer and promotion of officials under their control are 'directly ordered' by the CMs. Consequently, those affected can no longer hope to secure any relief by petitioning the heads of their service. Placed in such a predicament, a growing percentage of officers, whose careers are affected and family lives disrupted, are persuaded to shed their scruples and join the political bandwagon. Bereft of guidance and support from their superiors, functionaries at all levels are virtually compelled to come to terms with the harsh political realities of the environment in which they have to work, survive and get ahead.

In the earlier years, situations of this kind only marginally affected the functioning of IAS and IPS officers. This is no longer so. One of the reasons for the progressive decline of the all-India services is that in the past two decades and more, the career management of IAS and IPS officers has been sorely neglected by the Central authorities responsible for controlling the cadres of these services.

Yet another factor which has affected the management and functioning of the all-India service officers in the states is the visible decline in the standards and principles followed at the Centre. Irrespective of the mismanagement in the states, the Centre, not till long ago, was known for selecting and appointing the very best available officers to the top jobs. But not any longer. In recent years the Centre has been appointing non-select officers to the highest posts; granting multiple extensions to favoured officers and rewarding them with post-retirement assignments in India and abroad. The Centre having ceased to be the role model, state chief ministers no longer feel constrained to procure the required approvals of the Central authorities concerned in managing the state cadres. Such a deviation from the norm would have been unthinkable in the past.

It was Patel's vision that the all-India services, specially the IAS and IPS, would promote the unity of the country, enable valuable cross-fertilization of the administrative resource in the states and the Centre and provide the states a body of well-trained officers who would, being protected by the Centre, be able to withstand political or other pressures and efficiently run the administration in the states. The functioning of the political system in our country has most effectively negated Patel's concept.

Instead of using the all-India and the provincial services to carry their states rapidly towards socio-economic development, alleviation of poverty and maintenance of law and order and communal harmony, the chief ministers have politicized the cadres and used them as a handy tool for spreading nepotism, corruption and casteism. This has resulted in key appointments in many states – including the heads of autonomous institutions, universities and corporate bodies – being made on the basis of caste and community considerations. The service cadres have been splintered and groups of officers have emerged, known for their 'loyalty' to one or the other political party or faction. This perhaps explains the need for carrying out mass-scale transfers of functionaries in all departments at any time during the year or whenever there is a change of government or a Cabinet reshuffle, both phenomena being frequent occurrences in most states.

As a result of the politicization of the civil and police services, a grave danger faces the country. The liquidation of the established lines of command and control in governmental structures and public institutions, the spread of nepotism and corruption, and across-the-board loss of accountability have provided unfettered opportunities for criminal elements to thrive and engage in anti-national activities. This situation has been systematically exploited by the intelligence agencies of our adversaries which have established and spread their networks in several parts of the country to generate confusion and chaos.

The continuing lack of political stability at the Centre, virtually since 1989, has led to the executive becoming progressively ineffective. The numerical mix of the political parties represented in parliament has rendered it incapable of effectively exercising its mandated role of overviewing the functioning of the executive. The sharp decline in the functioning of both the executive and parliament has seen the ascendancy of the judiciary and the rise, in the recent past, of what has been popularly called 'judicial activism'.

The Supreme Court, the country's apex judicial institution, has been admitting public interest litigations (PIL) and issuing orders and directions to the state and Central governments to perform within specified time schedules. Some of these PIL cases have related to the failure of the authorities concerned to undertake effective removal of garbage and urban wastes to keep the cities clean; removal of industrial units from residential areas; eradicating sources of pollution and providing a liveable environment, etc.   ch interventions, directly relating to the role and responsibility of the executive, were unknown in the past. The public at large, unable to secure a response or redress from the government authorities or local self-governing bodies concerned, has been understandably elated with the verdicts of courts in cases involving omissions and commissions of the executive.

The interest and orders of the Supreme Court, and subsequently of the high courts, have embraced other public institutions, such as the functioning of the apex national crime investigation agency, the CBI. In the recent past, the CBI director was restrained from supervising the work of his juniors, one of whom was directed to report directly to the high court dealing with a particular case. While, in the short run, such orders may create enormous satisfaction among the public at large, they result in further weakening the already tottering command–and–control structures of important public institutions. Also, as has actually happened, once liberated from the superintendence of the higher governmental authorities, the CBI has been displaying proclivities of being answerable to none!

Thus, one great danger of the so–called judicial activism is that while it may seem to be filling the gap created by the failure of the executive and parliament, it may generate tendencies which have the potential of rendering the executive even more defunct than it has become via its own failures. The failures of the executive and parliament are beginning to create a situation which may result in also affecting the functioning of the judiciary.

Notwithstanding the failures on various fronts, it may be noted that the New Economic Policy (1991) and the consequent deregulation of the economic sector have shown that with reduced governmental controls there is reasonable basis for expecting enhanced investments, higher productivity and increasing rates of growth. The present situation indicates signs of the economy shaping up and, hopefully, leading to reduced foreign debt and fiscal deficit and comfortable foreign exchange reserves. The incipient successes on the economic front have led some to conclude that India has had far too much of government and, therefore, a contraction in its size shall, ipso facto, cure national governance of its various serious maladies. This line of argumentation appears naive, considering the deep-seated ills which afflict our society and polity.

The lot of hundreds of millions of our people, who live in poverty and neglect in remote rural areas and urban slums, cannot be expected to improve automatically merely by the states and the Centre reducing the size of their presence. As noted earlier, half of our population is still illiterate and we have miles to go to provide an acceptable standard of life to about one-third of our population which subsists below the poverty line. However, the recent upsurge on the economic front provides a reasonable basis to suggest that the very first step is to become competitive. Obviously, competition cannot be met by any business unit which is overstaffed, poorly directed, and in which the productivity of individuals is not measured. Efficiency, productivity and accountability are factors which have to be planned, strived for and secured. Thus, even if for no better reason than to achieve sustained economic growth of a higher order than in the past, we shall have to introduce and implement various reform measures. And for achieving the ideals ingrained in our Constitution and the objectives of a welfare state, we shall have to do very much more.

For far too long we have allowed the administrative apparatuses in the states to become no more than employing agencies, entities which provide jobs to the unemployed. Government offices and institutions are heavily overstaffed, mostly at the lower, non-decision-making levels. The procedures for taking disciplinary action against dishonest or delinquent officials are far too lengthy, time-consuming and, in most cases, ineffective. It is virtually impossible to get rid of the deadwood or to give preferential treatment to the more efficient and productive elements in the government machine. On top of this, we have imposed an elaborate system of reservations for various categories, both in initial recruitment and subsequent advancement. Further, the dishonest and irregular elements get protected and promoted instead of being thrown out. All in all, the head of a government department or public institution has inadequate control over his employees and his authority to punish or reward is seriously circumvented by elaborate, time-consuming procedures.

The situation as described above has also had its effect on the functioning of the IAS and IPS cadres. There are growing instances of dishonest and unprincipled functioning and, side by side, unscrupulous elements getting to the highest levels from where they further erode whatever is left of the erstwhile systems. Recently, chief secretaries, serving and retired, in at least three states, have been charged with serious irregularities and corruption. The number of senior civil servants against whom there are serious charges of omission and commission is also increasing in all states. Several directors-general of police, and a significant number of senior police officers, have been arrested for not functioning according to the law and a number of middle-ranking police officers are in jails, having been sentenced for custodial deaths and infringements of the law.

Senior government officials charged with acts of corruption or maladministration are not invariably convicted, nor in time. The position in respect of offenders among chief ministers, ministers and elected representatives holding public offices is even more unsatisfactory. Recent investigations by the CBI of several significant cases of alleged corruption and other serious offences have exposed the inadequacy of the existing anti-corruption laws. For one, assuming that there is no political interference in the work of the concerned investigation agencies, far too much time is lost in sanctions having to be procured before senior civil and police officers and members of the political executive can be proceeded against.

For the past three decades, the Central government has been talking about the establishment of a high-powered body at the Centre, called the Lokpal, to look into cases of corruption and maladministration involving the senior bureaucracy and ministers. Such a law still awaits enactment. Likewise, Lokayukts were proposed to be set up in the states. While this was done in several states, no results worth the mention have emerged so far from the functioning of these constitutional bodies. Recently, in Punjab, it was reported that the Lokayukt was on the threshold of ordering action against certain political personalities, on the basis of complaints investigated by it. However, before any judgment could be delivered or order passed, the state government issued an ordinance to scrap the institution of Lokayukt! So much for the political will to reduce or contain corruption.

Ever since the installation of the United Front government, in mid-1996, the Centre has been talking about the need for transparency in governmental functioning and the need to do away with excessive secrecy which informs the current systems; establishing a code of ethics in public life; better management of the civil services in the states by entrusting the responsibility for postings, transfers, etc., to a civil services board headed by the state chief secretary, and several other reforms. It remains to be seen whether these moves will fructify, how soon and to what effect. In this context, it may be recalled that the Centre had set up a National Police Commission (known as the Dharmavira Commission) which furnished eight reports (1979–81) on almost every facet of police functioning in the country. Despite the passage of many years, the states have refused to accept and implement the crucial recommendations of this Commission, especially the one relating to the mode of selection, appointment and tenure of the director general of police, on the brief ground that as 'police' and 'public order' are state subjects under the Constitution, the Centre should not seek to interfere in the autonomy of the states.

There is, however, growing public awareness about the malfunctioning of governments in the states and at the Centre. Thousands of non-governmental organizations (NGOs) have emerged, each seeking to improve one or the other facet of governmental functioning by exposing failures, corrupt practices and so on. So far only a limited number of these bodies have been able to do productive work. Also, fortunately, the coverage of the print and audio-visual media has increased considerably, almost all over the country. Newspapers, magazines and private television channels are quick to expose defaults and defalcations in the functioning of public organizations and services. While this has generated quick-fire trials by the media, it is hoped that balanced media reporting, preceded by the required hard work, will emerge in the coming years and be able to substantially support the public campaign against corruption and maladministration. Thus, this time around, at least some of the reformatory moves being made by the Centre, referred to above, may gain headway for no better reason than that failure to do so may generate criticism and confrontation on a scale which may be difficult to handle.

The people of our country live in villages and towns in the states. While the Centre, because of its larger responsibility, is duty bound to urgently initiate the various measures required to improve the governance of the country, it is equally necessary for each state to set about its own tasks. This should not be difficult as the political parties which run the states are fully aware of the failings of their public administration systems, having themselves created the existing chaos. However, on current reckoning, it does not appear likely that the existing polity in our country is concerned about the most urgent need to rid itself of greed and dishonesty and take a fresh vow to devotedly serve the people whom they represent.

Side by side, it cannot be reasonably expected that the bureaucracies shall cure themselves from within; they are bereft of the bold and selfless leadership which would be required to bring about any change. For the past few years, the younger members of the Uttar Pradesh IAS Association have been wanting to name the top three most corrupt officers in the state and have been successfully prevented from doing so by the strong vested interests among their ranks and outside. In this scenario, especially as the

Centre has grossly failed to provide the requisite support to officers of the all-India services in the states to stoutly oppose and refuse to carry out unlawful orders of their political masters, it would not do to presume that the functioning of the bureaucracies will improve on its own, in due course of time.

A remedy which has been frequently recommended for improving the governance of the country is to replace the cabinet system with the presidential form of government. Irrespective of the pros and cons of this approach, any move in this direction will require an amendment of the basic structure of the Constitution. On present reckoning, it does not seem possible that the political party mix in parliament will enable such a change to be carried through, especially considering the two-thirds majority vote required for bringing about such an alteration in the Constitution. Furthermore, since the Government of India Act of 1935, the people and political parties in our country have become increasingly conversant with the functioning of the parliamentary and cabinet systems. Successive prime ministers, from Nehru onwards, have taken care to provide representation in their cabinets to virtually every state and region and to the leaders of the various minority communities. Even so, we have still to see the satisfactory functioning of the existing system.

Replacing the present form of government with a directly elected president who, being unfettered, would be inclined to select his team of ministers on some other basis – ideally on considerations of experience, competence, honesty and so on – may lead to enormous difficulties in holding the country together. The experience of the United Front government (1996 onwards) has shown that the PM of a coalition government (representing a dozen and more regional parties) does not enjoy the freedom of selecting his ministers. The collaborating parties, who selected the PM, left him with virtually no choice of selecting his team. Against this background, it would seem far too simplistic to suggest that the only way out for securing sound governance of the country would relate to a constitutional change and imposition of a brand new system which may take a very long time to be understood and become acceptable to our polity and people.

Parliamentarians, leaders of political parties, political scientists, sociologists, journalists, social activists, thinkers and analysts have been proposing a variety of approaches to cure our society and polity and secure 'good' governance in India. While many of their recommendations could be seriously examined and implemented, especially those which relate to reform of the existing election law and processes and internal functioning of political parties, the very first step towards the restoration of sound governance and credibility of governmental functioning in the states and at the Centre would relate, more than any other single factor, to ensuring that the elected executive and the bureaucracies are visibly honest and function according to the Constitution and rule of law. If this can be done, the prospects of recovering the faith of the people and restoring their trust in governmental functioning would be high. This, in turn, will also see the restoration of efficiency, sensitivity, responsiveness and accountability – all of which are sadly lacking in the existing state of affairs.

Sustained adherence to ethical codes and value systems is a sine qua non of sound governance. Unfortunately, after the attainment of freedom, our educational system has altogether neglected the need to inculcate values and imbue the upcoming generations with any kind of idealism or spirit of nationalism. This grievous lapse has engendered a valueless society, which disregards ethical values, and a selfish, dishonest and parochial polity bereft of ideals and a national perspective. If the political leadership fails to act quickly, the existing mood of distrust, despondency and despair may very soon create a situation of chaos, confrontation and conflict, with grave consequences for national unity and the country's steady advancement towards mature nationhood.

15

The Rusting Steel Frame*

Since Independence, the country has achieved far-reaching developments on several fronts and the all-India Services (AIS) have contributed greatly to the progress achieved. In recent years, however, a large part of the blame for serious failures in various arenas has been attributed to the civil services – the nomenclature by which members of the AIS and all others comprising the administrative systems at the Centre and the states are generally referred to. Politicians, political scientists, economists, sociologists, analysts and journalists have been commenting on the country's problems and offering prescriptions on all that needs to be done to remedy the prevailing unsatisfactory governance of the country. It would be useful, perhaps necessary, to carefully consider the part so far played by the civil services in the complex tasks of nation building and to assess their usefulness in the years ahead. In this context, it would be relevant to at least briefly recount the genesis of the AIS, as they have so far been considered the leading services.

Of subcontinental dimensions, our country is a land of variegated splendour – permanently snow-clad mountain ranges, deserts, plains, islands and a very long coastline. India has 4,599 communities which speak 325 languages and dialects in twelve

---

* First published in V.N. Narayanan and Jyoti Sabharwal (eds.), *India at 50 – Bliss of Hope and Burden of Reality*, New Delhi: Sterling Publishers, 1997.

distinct language families and practise different religions. Each area has its own deep-rooted culture and lifestyle.

India has not always been administered by a central authority. With the promulgation of the Regulation Act in 1772, the British commenced the process to exercise control over the fast-spreading influence and the expanding coffers of the East India Company. In course of time, the entire country was subjugated and effective administrative control established. The first generation of administrators, the pioneers or the founders as they were called, were picked up by the British from among the commercial echelons and the army. Consequently, the early years of the colonial rule saw merchants, traders and soldiers assuming the role of district officers, magistrates and judges. In subsequent years some of them emerged as well-known governors of provinces and statesmen – Munro, Malcolm, Elphinstone, Metcalfe and the Lawrence brothers to name a few. The pioneers worked very hard, under extremely trying physical conditions in most cases. They settled the newly conquered territories, resolved political issues, enforced law and order, assessed and collected land revenue, administered civil and criminal justice, constructed canals, roads and bridges and managed schools and hospitals – in fact, did whatever was required to be done in the areas entrusted to their charge.

An effective takeover by the Crown followed the Mutiny of 1957. A covenanted service, the Indian Civil Service (ICS) was established to man the vital posts in the provinces and at the seats of the imperial authority. Posts of lesser importance were manned by the uncovenanted services. Members of the ICS, who enjoyed immense authority and exercised it arrogantly, were variously described as 'heaven-born', 'little Napoleons', 'the steel frame'.

To consolidate their hegemony in the annexed areas, the British created provinces which were ruled by governors; other territories were placed under the charge of chief commissioners. In the period up to 1935, the map of India was shaped by military, political and administrative exigencies of the moment, without regard to the affinities or aspirations of the people.

With the passage of the Government of India Act in 1935, provincial autonomy was ushered in and steps were taken towards establishing a federal system of governance. The British did not consider it necessary to establish a new cadre to man the posts in the Central government. They created the post of an establishment officer (EO) in 1936, and made him responsible for the selection and appointment of ICS officers to man the 'strategic' posts in the various departments and ministries in Delhi. To provide the EO with the necessary clout, he was positioned in the finance ministry. A major responsibility of the EO was to closely follow and assess the overall requirements of senior jobs in the provinces and at the Centre (undersecretary upwards); to notify the Central vacancies to the provinces; to watch the performance of officers in the provinces and to identify those with high potential to serve at the Centre; and assist a high-level collegiate committee to make final selections for appointment to various posts at the Centre, with the approval of the governor general.

After the inauguration of provincial autonomy, the British reduced the then existing nine AIS to three, retaining the ICS, Indian Police (IP) and Indian Medical Service (IMS). The ICS ceased to be members of the governor's executive council, which was replaced by the council of ministers. ICS officers also ceased to be members of the provincial legislatures. From exercising unfettered authority, the ICS was now required to give greater attention to the functioning of the village panchayats, cooperative societies and district boards. Many British ICS officers resigned and left. Those who chose to tolerate and work under the elected Indian representatives remained to serve.

In 1947, when India attained freedom, serious problems and complex challenges faced the government. The British had ruled the country to safeguard and promote their own interests. Their legacy was a backward and feudal agrarian economy, an extremely weak industrial base, gross unemployment and abysmally low incomes. The economy, which had serious imbalances, provided hardly any scope for capital formation, much less for investment opportunities.

The tasks before the nation were indeed of a gargantuan scale. In the months preceding Independence, there were organized communal rioting and untold violence in several parts of the country; tens of thousands of innocent persons were massacred. With the sudden departure of British and Muslim officials, the administrative machinery had been seriously disrupted. There were serious shortages of essential supplies, especially of foodgrains. Millions of refugees and displaced persons had to be fed, clothed and provided medical care and shelter. Rioting and lawlessness continued – shops, offices and houses were being looted and burnt. The threat of another famine loomed large. Before the government at the Centre could settle down to its innumerable tasks, Pakistan invaded Kashmir.

It was against this background that decisions had to be taken about the system of public administration and how free India would be governed. Almost all the front-ranking Indian leaders looked upon the ICS officers, even the Indians among them, with distrust and suspicion. Jawaharlal Nehru was quite clearly opposed to the continuation of the administrative machinery bequeathed by the British. As the leader of the interim government, he had clearly stated that a new order could not be created as long as the authoritarian spirit of the ICS pervaded the public administration. He was of the unambiguous view that the ICS and the other AIS must completely disappear before 'we can start real work on a new order'.

Vallabhbhai Patel was, however, strongly opposed to Nehru's perceptions; it was his conviction that the ICS had been an efficient service. During the debates in the Constituent Assembly, he argued in favour of retaining the AIS to build independent India. He convened a provincial premiers' conference, in October 1946, to evolve a consensus on the future of AIS. His reasoning was that besides the Centre, the provinces would also require competent officers to deal with new and complex tasks. The opportunity of working in the districts would provide the AIS officers with practical experience, the opportunity of contact with the people and awareness of the situation obtaining in the country and 'their practical experience would be most useful to them'. Such officers could be drawn to serve the Centre on deputation, as during the pre-Independence period. This would enable them to gain 'different experience and wider outlook in a larger sphere. A combination of these experiences would make the services more efficient. They will also serve as a liaison between the provinces and the Central government and introduce certain amount of vigour in the administration both of the Centre and the provinces.' He, therefore, exhorted the premiers: 'My advice is that we should have all-India services.'

Speaking in the Constituent Assembly, Patel stressed: 'You will not have a united India if you do not have a good all-India service,' with the independence to speak its mind and which enjoy a sense of security. He went to the extent of warning: 'If you do not adopt this course, then do not follow this Constitution … this Constitution is meant to be worked by a ring of service which will keep the country intact … these people are the instrument … remove them and I see nothing but a picture of chaos all around the country.' Patel's views were opposed by Nehru and G.B. Pant. Some of the provinces were also unhappy and preferred to have their own superior services. Despite the opposition, Patel succeeded in securing a decision to retain AIS.

In providing for AIS, the objectives of the founding fathers were to facilitate liaison between the Centre and the states, and enable the maintenance of a certain level of uniformity in standards of administration all over the country. They also wanted to enable the Centre to keep in touch with the ground realities in the states; to enable the administrative apparatus in the states to acquire a broader outlook; to provide the states with the best available talent for running their administration; and finally, to see that political considerations were not allowed to operate in the recruitment, discipline and control of AIS officers.

Our Constitution provides for the establishment of the AIS. The states also have the right to form their own civil services. Consequently, the Indian Administrative Service (IAS) and the Indian Police Service (IPS) were created under the All-India Services Act, 1951. The Constitution provides that other AIS can also be created by resolutions of parliament if it is necessary or expedient to do so in the national interest. In 1961, parliament had passed a resolution to create three more AIS: Indian Service of Engineers, Indian Medical and Health Service and Indian Forest Service. The constitution of the first two was thwarted on the ground that it infringed the autonomy of the states. However, the Indian Forest Service came into being in 1966.

To attract the best talent, members of the AIS are recruited on an all-India basis and enjoy specified pay scales and privileges. To provide members of the AIS security against political pulls and pressures, they are placed under the ultimate control of the Union even though they are allocated to state-wise cadres and function under the control of the state governments, unless on deputation to the Centre.

Our Constitution seeks to secure justice – social, economic and political – to all its citizens. The Directive Principles of State Policy provide the framework for national reconstruction and all-round development, especially the upliftment of the economically depressed and socially oppressed segments of our society. The Constitution also provides the basis for a common framework of governance through a uniform set of interrelated institutions legitimized by the fundamental law of the land. While the areas of governance are demarcated between the Union and the states, the founding fathers of our Constitution perceived the need for a strong Centre to guide and support the states in the common endeavour of nation building.

As the vast majority of our people live in the villages, the efficient implementation of developmental programmes in the states is understandably of vital importance. Even though the responsibilities of the Union and the states stand demarcated, the effective functioning of our federal system depends on the pursuit of a national perspective. It was Patel's vision that such a perspective, and the very unity of India, could be secured through a federal administrative system in which the AIS would play a crucial role. In 1949, looking back over the events since 1947, Patel complimented the civil services for their ability and patriotism. Stressing, yet again, that there could not be a substitute for the AIS, he observed, 'If most of the officers had not behaved patriotically and with loyalty, the Union would have collapsed.'

Besides the creation of a federal administrative system, it was also decided to adopt a planned economy to secure balanced economic growth and social development. The mechanics of national economic planning were expected to provide another unifying force to enable a coordinated approach and joint action by the Union and the states. The establishment of the Planning Commission and the National Development Council were in furtherance of this approach. As observed earlier, the British configured the country's map to safeguard their own interests – gain quick profits, support the industry in England and keep India dependent. Raw materials were exported and industrial growth thwarted. Consequently, there was sharp unevenness in the levels of economic development and availability of financial resources in the various provinces. There were similar imbalances in the princely states which were controlled by the Doctrine of Paramountcy. Thus, in 1947, besides the problems relating to the serious economic imbalances, the government was required to deal with difficulties arising from two vastly differing politico-administrative cultures in the provinces and the princely states.

Despite these and numerous other constraints, the civil services of the day worked with determination to tackle the post-1947 challenges which included resettling millions of refugees, restoring law and order, establishing and running thousands of depots to distribute food and other items of scarce supply (which were rationed), fighting floods and drought. The foremost priority was to meet the problems of poverty and unemployment and the challenges of socio-economic development. The administrative system was required to undertake organized programmes of community development. Both on account of paucity of resources and to promote self-reliance, people's participation was given high importance in the implementation of developmental programmes. Thus emerged the importance of development administration. It was also recognized that orderly change and stability would act as a bulwark against social unrest and violence.

Considering the size of our country, its galloping population and innumerable problems on various fronts, it could be said that for the first nearly three decades the country made steady progress. This period witnessed the expansion of education and health facilities, emergence of universities and centres of scientific and technological learning and research, establishment of agricultural research institutions and universities, and expansion of highways, railways and public transport. It also witnessed giant strides on the food production front, paving the way for the success of the Green Revolution. Considerable headway was achieved in carrying out land reforms, providing security of tenure to the actual tillers and consolidation of holdings: construction of large dams and expansion of irrigation systems which, in turn, made the Green Revolution possible. Industrial development proceeded apace and progress was also achieved in expanding power generation, increasing steel and cement production and infrastructural development. The Atomic Energy Commission contributed to nuclear power generation and application of atomic energy for medical treatment, preservation of foodgrains and many other peaceful purposes. During this period, the country faced foreign aggression on three occasions; while we had to accept humiliation in 1962, our armed forces acquitted themselves with honour in the 1965 and 1971 conflicts. Thus, while deficiencies remained on several fronts, it can be said that, overall, our country was well set on the path of progress.

One reason for the governance of the country being on an even keel during this period was that a large majority of the first-generation political leadership, who comprised the Central and state Cabinets, were persons who had participated in the freedom struggle and made large sacrifices. Most of them were highly educated and imbued with a nationalist ideology and perspective. Their known public reputation for honesty and high ethical values gave them the stature to lead the administrative structures in the states and the Centre, and command respect from the people they served. The fact that the same political party was at the helm in the Centre and the states provided an added advantage; the state chief ministers had access to the Centre and old links helped to resolve many problems. In any case, the states were not in confrontation with the Union.

From the late 1960s onwards, the Congress started facing internal problems. The quality of leadership had started declining and internal feuds and power politics were gaining ascendancy. Indira Gandhi's decision not to yield authority at any cost led to the enforcement of Emergency in the country (1975–77). In this period, rule by law and the Constitution suffered great damage. Important decisions were taken in utter disregard of the cabinet system and executed by 'loyal' officers. 'Committed' civil servants, some of them known for their doubtful integrity, joined the political bandwagon to advance their individual interests, their gross felonies being protected by those whom they served. While corruption and maladministration was not unknown in the earlier years, the Emergency witnessed extralegal elements playing a dominant role, providing a linkage between corrupt politicians and unprincipled civil servants.

The end of Emergency saw the ouster of the Congress. The party was back in power in 1980 and, thereafter, ruled at the Centre till 1996, except during the relatively brief tenures of the V.P. Singh and Chandra Shekhar governments. The United Front government took over in mid-1996. Meanwhile, however, the Congress lost power in many of the major states.

Irrespective of the political party which has been in power in the states in the past two decades, the standards of governmental functioning have witnessed continuing decline. Side by side, there has also been deterioration in the functioning of the Centre. Besides serious problems of internal security, manifested by militancy, terrorism and repeated disturbance of the public order, there has been an enormous increase in complaints of corruption and maladministration in recent years. The IAS and IPS have suffered loss of credibility. Today, almost all over the country, there is a general perception that all public servants are dishonest, demanding and insensitive to the interests of the people they serve.

Since 1994, there has been an unending spate of exposures of corruption. These scandals involved allegations against a former prime minister and several of his cabinet ministers, and serving or retired senior civil servants. Also, there have been cases alleging gross abuse of authority in the states, involving chief ministers, ministers and the senior-most echelons of the civil services and police. Several former ministers at the Centre have already been convicted by the highest court of the land and a good number of them are facing prosecution. A good number of police officers in the states, including several directors general of police, are undergoing investigation for serious criminal offences and gross abuse of authority: some of them are serving jail sentences. Likewise, several former chief secretaries and senior civil servants are under investigation for serious charges and a number of IAS officers are being dealt with for corruption.

In Uttar Pradesh, officers of the IAS cadre went on a prolonged agitation for the identification of the 'most corrupt' among their senior-most officers, to be followed by their prosecution. This was, indeed, a most distressing situation considering that until recently this state produced the most eminent political leaders and some of the best-known civil servants. Bihar, which too produced some of the best-known political leaders and public servants, also stands deeply enmeshed in serious problems of corruption, maladministration, and open caste and class wars. The situation in other states is also providing cause for serious concern.

The continuing failure of the executive at the Centre and in the states has led to the emergence of social activist groups which seek to combat corruption, maladministration, delays, inefficiencies et al., in their respective styles. Side by side, there has been a steady increase in the number of public interest litigations in the higher courts against the failures of governments. Some of these cases are targeted against corruption in the highest levels of authority. Arising from these cases, the Supreme Court has passed strictures against the Central government and awarded punitive sentences to two former Union cabinet ministers. Taking the cue from the apex court, several high courts and even lower courts have been awarding exemplary punishments in cases involving ministers and civil and police officers.

On the economic front, the country has witnessed sustainable progress after the launch of the New Economic Policy in 1991. The deregulation of systems and procedures in the arena of industry and commerce has undoubtedly led to a spurt of initiatives yielding higher export earnings, enlarging our foreign exchange reserves and, generally, establishing the country's economic standing. An argument has been repeatedly raised in the recent past that we have far too much of 'government' in almost every area of functioning and that reducing the same will lead to improved efficiency, promptness and honesty in the delivery of services, especially those which involve the welfare of the common man. Further, it is being said that the AIS have failed miserably, and greater good will emerge if they are wound up, or at least their size and responsibility significantly curtailed.

While close and urgent attention needs to be given to all our major problems, the time has come to critically assess and arrive at an objective judgement whether the evolution of our democracy and the socio-economic development of our country has achieved a level of development which lends itself to a reduction in the role of public administration in dealing with the task of nation building.

A quick look at the country's current standing would show that we have not so far made headway in containing the burgeoning growth of our population; we are not halfway through in achieving the target of 100 per cent literacy; while assessments vary, several hundred million of our people still live below the poverty line; the rate of growth of agricultural production is low and unsteady; our food stocks are dwindling; millions are yet to gain employment; there are severe shortages of power supply and our infrastructure development is lagging behind; we have a large public debt and a growing fiscal deficit.

Considering the continuing complaints and growing public dissatisfaction over the levels of corruption and malfunctioning of the administrative machinery in the states, and recently at the Centre, a criticism which is now being frequently voiced is that the AIS concept is obsolete; officers of these services are dishonest, inefficient and indifferent; they are mixed up with corrupt politicians and criminal elements; there is no special advantage in retaining the AIS.

These are not altogether baseless. However, they do not bring out the full picture of the malaise which has struck governmental functioning in recent years.

Over the years, governance through known policies, systems, rules and procedures has been vitiated by political interference and all kinds of extra-constitutional pulls and pressures. Successive elections in the states, and of late also at the Centre, have not invariably thrown up clear majorities. State governments run by chief ministers representing faction-ridden parties commanding slender majorities, or coalitions, are unable to exert their will, assuming that those serving as chief ministers have any vision and requisite competence to provide direction to their administrations.

To remain in power at any cost, the political executives consciously select pliable officers. In filling up important posts in the state administrative set-up, high consideration is also given to the caste, ethnicity and political affinities of potential incumbents.

Thus, over time, the state cadres of all public services, including the AIS, have been politicized and communalized with resultant inefficiency, indiscipline and unaccountability. The manner in which appointments and promotions are made in the states has resulted in eliminating those who have no political support or linkages and whose only recommendation is their seniority, competence, experience and integrity. Very few officers of the latter category get the appointments they deserve. Instead, they are assigned to peripheral jobs, and waste away. This has generated loss of morale and cynicism.

The manner of appointments to field jobs, especially the posts of district magistrate (DM) and superintendent of police (SP) and the tenures allowed to them are matters for most serious concern. Relatively young officers posted in the districts are transferred on the slightest excuse, in most cases for not having acted as per the diktats of the local MLA, MP or one of the ministers from the area, or for annoying a politically connected individual or coterie. Officers shifted from one district may land up in another or to a non-job at the state headquarters. Besides disrupting the local administration and adversely affecting the development process, frequent transfers of key district officers result in the disruption of their training, demoralization, demotivation and an overall feeling of insecurity. Frequent shifts, at times within a few days of taking over in a district, adversely affect the family life of those moved, especially the education of their children. In many cases, the sudden transfer of an officer also results in the spouse losing her/his job.

Appointments to key district jobs are not invariably made from among a batch of officers who have the requisite seniority, experience and reputation for good work and honesty. At times, several batches may be overlooked to favour a junior and ineligible officer and give him a coveted field job. There are also instances of IAS and IPS officers, who enjoy political patronage, becoming veteran field functionaries by doing full tenures in several districts when some of their batchmates have not been afforded a single posting as DM or SP. Young officers, fresh from the civil services and police training academies, on joining their allotted state cadres, have to quickly commence the process of unlearning. Within a few years of service they get wiser, having imbibed the mechanics of survival. Such reorientation breeds cynicism, indifference and a virtual disregard for the rule of law. The situation in regard to postings of heads of departments and to senior positions in the state secretariat is no different.

While premature and frequent transfers on the basis of political consideration are resorted to in almost all states, Uttar Pradesh is perhaps the worst offender in this regard. In this context, it may be recalled that during the British period, Vallabhbhai Patel wanted the DM of Gurgaon (in the erstwhile Punjab province) to be transferred out. Patel's appeals in the matter, successively addressed to the Punjab governor and the viceroy, were rejected!

The political leadership in the states has, over the years, amply demonstrated that it is not obligated to follow the laid-down systems and procedures. Successive state chief ministers, even the better among them, have been running the administrative apparatus through patronage, rewarding pliant officers through attractive postings and unmerited promotions for services rendered in the past or expected in the future. The quid pro quo for such rewards is collection of funds for the politicians in power and keeping their supporters satisfied. This pattern of administration has resulted in virtually liquidating the very basis of accountability of organizations and individual functionaries. No principled senior functionary would dare to question the irregularities being committed by an officer below him if the latter has direct political links. Besides breeding maladministration and corruption, this has led to the ruination of the administrative structures and growing indiscipline.

The politicization of public services, with money and muscle power playing an increasing role, has negated the scope of orderly functioning. With the unseemly elements in all the public services, including the AIS, being fully protected against any questioning, the concept of accountability and responsibility has become defunct.

In the past, up to the end of Indira Gandhi's first tenure as prime minister, effective public administration was looked upon as a vital instrument for implementing time-bound socio-economic development goals and providing prompt and satisfactory responses to the needs and aspirations of the masses. However, even during Nehru's long tenure as prime minister, cracks had started developing in the public administration system. Partap Singh Kairon (a renowned chief minister of Punjab) and Bakshi Ghulam Mohammad (chief minister of J&K) were pioneers in establishing the philosophy of 'getting along with the job and showing speedy results', even if this meant giving all established systems the go-by. Their highly personalized and altogether unconventional styles of administration, operating through a handful of selected officials who were at liberty to disregard the laid-down systems, drove the first nails in the coffin of accountability. It is another matter that both of them were indicted by high-level commissions of inquiry and both had to step down. However, their successes in achieving quick results led to their functional styles being emulated by latter-day chief ministers and further damage was done to organizations and systems.

The national civil services and police training academies imbue probationers with the need to remain politically neutral and maintain objectivity and anonymity. However, the administrative environment has been grossly vitiated by the ferocious competition among the various political parties, which are ever-increasing in number. The acute politicization of the public administrative system and the continuing turmoil and turbulence in society have adversely effected the functioning of public services. The existing socio-political realities are totally bereft of any value system or the need for adherence to any ethical code in public life. Needless to say, this has not left the services, including the AIS, untouched.

In the earlier years, the majority of AIS officers in the state cadres were direct recruits to the services and enjoyed considerable homogeneity and camaraderie. With the passage of time, the AIS cadres have grown excessively large and now comprise direct recruits, officers promoted to IAS and IPS from among the state services, former emergency commissioned officers from the army, and lateral entrants. The erstwhile esprit de corps has disappeared and there is no internal solidarity in the cadres. The cadres are, in fact, divided into various groups based on community, caste, ethnic and other affinities. With chief secretaries and directors general of police being appointed on the basis of political considerations, there are no longer any role models to be emulated. The AIS cadres in the states are virtually leaderless and perforce look outside their fold for support and guidance.

The AIS are controlled by the Centre: IAS by the Department of Personnel, IPS by the home ministry, and IFoS by the Ministry of Environment. Over the years, with political considerations playing a dominant role, the Central cadre-controlling authorities have not been able to enforce the requisite control over the state authorities. In matters relating to cadre management, the state governments no longer act according to the service rules or after consulting the Centre. For instance, almost every state has created, with impunity, unauthorised ex-cadre posts at the senior-most levels. Resultantly, a state of the size of Punjab may have half a dozen or more IAS officers enjoying the pay scale earlier available only to the chief secretary and an equal number of IPS officers enjoying the remuneration permissible to the DGP! Because of the tenuous nature of Centre–state relations, and political considerations being foremost, the state authorities indulge in serious deviations from the All India Service Rules and the Central authorities concerned can do no better than issue communications, pointing out the irregularities committed by the states concerned.

The Centre's role stands diluted for other reasons also. In recent years, there have been instances of IAS officers who were not empanelled to serve as secretaries being appointed to the highest post of cabinet secretary. The Centre has also not been following a consistent policy in granting extensions to retiring officers. Further, officers of unproven mettle and doubtful vintage have been elevated to high constitutional posts, thus sending a signal that seniority, competence and integrity stand discounted. These and other deviations from the norm at the Centre have emboldened the state governments to follow similar irregular approaches in rewarding officers whom they find useful.

In sum, the broad picture before us today is that all public services in the states, including the AIS, stand politicized, communalized and exploited. The approaches to appointments, promotions, tenures and transfers being followed by the state chief ministers seldom permit the best available officers, of proven competence and known integrity, to occupy the highest jobs, especially those of chief secretary and DGP. With weak-kneed, pliant and even officers of uncertain integrity being elevated to these vital posts, there is just no scope for the heads of the civil and police services taking positions, adequately protecting their flock, and thwarting illegal directions and interference. Being absorbed in their own interests and post-retirement prospects, these officers are unconcerned when the secretariats under their charge roll out, day after day, orders affecting the interests of subordinate personnel whose performance and welfare they are expected to guide and safeguard.

In most cases, they seek to explain away their position by asserting that the 'orders have been directly issued by the chief minister'. The officers who are victimized or subjected to harassment of one or the other kind – denied due promotion, ignored for a particular appointment despite being the senior-most eligible candidate, denied training opportunities, subjected to repeated transfers, placed under unwarranted inquiry, or suspension, etc. – cannot expect protection or support from the CS or DGP. Often, officers who have grievances seek the help of political personalities or influential businessmen to plead their cases with the chief minister and get them relief. This has led to further politicization of the cadres, generated indiscipline and created a situation in which the well-established command–and–control structures have become redundant and further eroded the enforcement of accountability.

The political executives running the state governments are well aware of the mess they have created. However, they are compelled by their own limited concerns of staying in power at any cost. They seek to have their day-to-day interests served and their behests carried out without questioning. Their political interests are well served by selective utilization of the administrative machinery, operating through their 'own' officers placed in key positions in the field and the state secretariat. Thus they have no interest in ensuring that their administrations run efficiently and honestly.

Such an approach to administration was earlier known only in the states; in the last few years, the functioning at the Centre has shown similar proclivities. With a very slender majority, the Congress government (1991–96) was also compelled by considerations of survival. Beset by charges of failure and allegations of corruption, the Rao government was ill-placed to question the states about the growing aberrations in the functioning of their administrative machineries, much less call their conduct to account. The coalition governments that succeeded the Rao government at the Centre were in an even weaker position to undertake the kind of initiatives which could result in reform.

All that we have today is almost a continuing public debate on the need for 'good governance' in the country. A remedy often recommended is to amend the Constitution and provide for a presidential form of government, replacing the Cabinet system. It is argued that this will introduce the much-needed honesty and accountability in the functioning of political and bureaucratic echelons. Irrespective of the merits of this argument, the present configuration of parliament does not permit the possibility of any change being introduced in the existing Constitution. Any alteration of its basic structure would require the mandatory support of a two-thirds majority.

The prospect of the public services curing themselves from within is bleak. While we still have extremely competent officers of firm convictions and high moral stature in almost every public service, including a large number in the AIS, it would not be practical to expect that individuals or small groups of officers dispersed all over our large country can effectively thwart the ill-conceived approaches of the political executives in the states. The scope of such a move being successfully made by officers serving at the Centre would perhaps be equally limited. In recent years, individual officers who have shown courage and refused to do wrong have not received the support of their peers and superiors. Such sporadic examples cannot snowball into movements unless they receive very strong and unified support from the services at large. After brief complimentary references in the media, such officers have not been heard of again.

Notwithstanding all this, there are rays of hope on several fronts. A large number of social and activist groups have emerged all over the country. Among their various concerns is the need for securing accountability of governmental functioning at all levels and honest and efficient delivery of public services. Such NGOs are also exposing cases of dishonesty and corruption and focusing public attention on the misdeeds of politicians and public servants.

Side by side with social activism targeted at the quality of governance, there is growing public awareness of the obligation of government authorities to protect and safeguard fundamental human rights. In this regard, the National Human Rights Commission (NHRC), set up in 1994, has done outstanding work in exposing the serious deficiencies which obtain in various areas of functioning. The manner in which our jails and police departments work has received special attention and based on the findings or directions of the NHRC, a number of serving police officers and others are already undergoing imprisonment. While the number of officials dealt with by the NHRC may be a very small percentage of the total strength of the bureaucracy, a signal has gone out about the fate which awaits those who choose to act unlawfully or commit wrongs. Over a period, the functioning of the NHRC is bound to have a salutary effect on the functioning of various organizations and, in the process, compel reform and prudent exercise of authority.

Another encouraging opening has been provided by the orders passed by the Supreme Court in various public interest litigation (PIL) cases in which allegations of maladministration and corruption were made against ministers and senior civil servants. The severe punishments awarded by the apex court in some of these cases should also result in cautioning all those who choose to exercise authority wantonly. While it may be unwise to expect the judiciary to bear the mantle of reforming the executive, judicial activism in glaring cases of default by public authorities should have a chastising effect, at least in the short run.

In our democratic system, the press has a vital role. While there has been large-scale expansion of the print and visual media in recent years, a focused approach to dealing with major societal and political issues has still to evolve. There is, as yet, excessive and exaggerated coverage of exposures and scandals and far too little well-informed comment or analysis of the various deep-rooted factors which generate the continuing malaise. The media could make an extremely useful contribution by devoting adequate coverage to tasks well done, highlighting the achievements of honest and efficient public servants and organizations, according special attention to developments in the remote and backward areas of our country. Our media is free and unfettered. It should be able to expose cases and incidents involving irregular and unlawful exercise of authority and abuses of all kinds. The existing ills in our socio-political environment will, on present reckoning, take considerable time to remedy. All processes of change are time-consuming.

But we cannot wait indefinitely for the desired changes to come about on their own. We face extremely serious internal security problems – communal tensions and violence, organized crime, militancy and terrorism. Millions of our people are illiterate, unemployed, impoverished, sick and shelter-less, and survive below the poverty line. Our population is increasing apace and economic inequities are continuing. Unless the Central and state governments take effective steps to improve the existing state of affairs in time, the country may face chaos, turbulence and serious unrest in the years ahead. Such an eventuality could seriously destabilize the established authority and even result in fracturing the integrity of the Union. It is thus most urgent and essential that the public administration systems become efficient, responsive, productive, honest and accountable. For this to happen, political and extralegal interference has to end.

Recently, the Department of Personnel and Administrative Reforms has circulated papers and organized a series of meetings all over the country to focus on the needed administrative reforms. Among the recommended approaches is a proposal to establish civil services boards in the states to be responsible for all personnel matters – appointments, postings, transfers, tenures, etc. – without political interference. Another relates to the adoption of a code of ethics to be followed by those involved in public functioning. Prima facie, both of these appear to be sound and relevant approaches. Too much time should not be lost in refining these concepts. Further improvements can be made after gaining experience of their application in the near future.

As per the constitutional position, the Centre cannot issue a directive to the states to enforce the aforesaid or other similar reformatory moves. A quick, practical way out would perhaps be for the prime minister to convene a special meeting with all the chief ministers to educate them about the extremely serious consequences which lie ahead if they continue with their existing styles of functioning and bring them around, pressurising if necessary (as Patel did years ago), to a clear commitment to mend their ways. Such an objective cannot be achieved by writing letters or issuing emotional appeals.

The prime minister would also need to consider time-bound steps for cases of corruption to be dealt with promptly and effectively. Experience has shown that failure to prosecute dishonest public servants has adversely affected the overall functioning and marred the public images of the services to which the offenders belong and created the general impression that the government is not interested in checking corruption. Despite the passage of over three decades, the establishment of Lokpal and Lokayukts has still to materialize. No more time should be lost in establishing effective mechanisms to deal with cases of corruption and maladministration, especially with the felonies of civil servants at all levels.

The country will continue to need honest and efficient public services for many years to come. Let us not waste time in beguiling ourselves that the awaited fruits of globalization and deregulation shall, by introducing competitiveness in the marketplace, also result in curing our society and polity of its existing ills. The problems of nearly two-thirds of our people, who live in more than half a million villages, demand our most urgent attention. We have to also care for the millions upon millions who live in most distressing circumstances in urban slums. The lot of our poor and impoverished people cannot and will not improve just by our leaders mouthing populist slogans or the public services promising to behave better.

Our public services have to work very hard and honestly, like the founders and pioneers of the British days did, to achieve the much-needed results. There should be no doubt in any quarter that the country will continue to require efficient and honest public services of various kinds. In the past five decades and more, the IAS and IPS have, despite aberrations of one kind or the other, acted as unifying forces and rendered notable services to the nation. The AIS shall continue to be needed in the trying times ahead.

We have no time to lose in systematically tackling the serious tasks of building a strong, self-reliant, prosperous and truly democratic India, fully protected from any onslaught, from within or without. It is necessary that the elected representatives and the public services work closely together and urgently devote themselves to meeting the challenges which face the country.

16

Corruption and the Indian Polity*

It is not my aim here to trace the origins and growth of corruption in India, nor its manifestation in every sphere of human activity, but to briefly reflect upon the progressive spread of corruption in the governance of free India.

To be corrupted is to be tainted, which can take a thousand forms. Simply stated, corruption implies lack of integrity, disloyalty, resort to bribery or any dishonest practice and moral debasement or depravity of one or the other kind. While deception and deceit may be considered to be contemporaneous with the emergence of homo sapiens, the incidence of dishonesty in the early human settlements was almost unknown, essentially because these incipient societies were small, self-regulated and, in conformity with their rough and ready codes of conduct, offenders were subjected to swift and severe punishment.

Corruption, in the sense that it is understood today, emerged as a serious aberration when societies started getting larger, societal conduct assumed greater complexity, and the structures of governance started regulating human activities. The evolution of civil societies was marked by the regulation of human conduct and interpersonal and inter-institutional dealings within the framework of civil, criminal and other laws. The society at large was expected

---

* First published in *Denouement*, December 1999.

to conform to given value systems and codes of conduct. Looking back, it would appear that the regulations and systems evolved to impart objectivity and fairness to mechanisms of governance did not invariably achieve this objective. Experience has shown that the exercise of regulatory authority actually contributed to an increase in corruption in various spheres of administrative control and enforcement.

Corruption in public life and governmental functioning was not unknown during British rule. However, it was not widespread largely because political and economic activities were restricted and kept under close watch by the rulers.

The long struggle for securing freedom was spearheaded by tall leaders who were known for their nationalistic fervour, proven integrity, ideological convictions and uncompromising principles. The majority of them had sacrificed their personal and family interests for the national cause. Some, like Mahatma Gandhi, had even renounced their hearth and home with single-minded devotion to the struggle and many others had happily gifted all their material belongings to support the liberation movement.

When India attained freedom, eminent political personalities, most of whom had spent long years in British jails, adorned the Cabinets in the states and the Centre. When the new governments were installed, the state chief ministers and the prime minister of India reiterated their commitment to provide the people of India with clean and honest administration, improve the lot of the teeming millions, secure equitable socio-economic development and build a strong and vibrant nation. These aspirations were later embodied in the Constitution.

It was the dedication, hard work and unquestionable integrity of the front-ranking political leaders that enabled the country, immediately after Partition, to successfully meet gigantic challenges. During this period, in which were laid the foundations of our democracy and advance towards nation building, corruption, nepotism and maladministration had started growing. Among the numerous complaints and allegations at least two chief ministers faced serious charges of nepotism and dishonest functioning – Bakshi Ghulam Mohammed (J&K) and Pratap Singh Kairon (Punjab). Even though Prime Minister Nehru had a soft corner for the two political leaders, for their go-getting style in steering their states towards rapid development, both of them had to step down after high-level probes found them guilty. Looking back, it could be said that they were among the pioneers in institutionalizing corruption.

The political developments in the late 1960s and the resultant instability saw the emergence of power politics, a new species of brazenness and determination not to yield power at any cost which, soon enough, saw the promulgation of Emergency in the country. Political instability and a progressive decline in values have over the years seen the degradation of the parliamentary system, damage to the functioning of the Cabinet and disregard of the Constitution and the rule of law. Another serious consequence has been the continuing erosion of the integrity of the civil services and a new breed of 'committed' bureaucracy.

In the past two decades, there has been a mushrooming of parties of varied hues – over 550 are registered with the Election Commission of India. Those which managed to assume power have been engaged not in grappling with the serious tasks of governance but in perennially gathering funds. As elections are contested not on the basis of issues or ideologies but by seeking to influence voters through monetary attractions and a variety of pressures, the electoral process has become increasingly expensive, debased and criminalized.

Money and muscle power play a vital role and no honest and experienced person can think of contesting elections at any level unless he has considerable financial backing or very large personal resources. Power politics and the lack of consensus among the major parties even in regard to issues of the highest national concern has led to the frequent fall of governments, necessitating fresh polls every other year. The 1999 parliamentary elections were the third in four years! The frequency of elections has seen the fund gathering machineries working with devastating vigour, displaying remarkable ingenuity in devising newer mechanisms to achieve their targets.

From beseeching and soliciting contributions towards their election funds in the earlier years, political parties have since progressed to demanding and even extorting payments. Since collections, cuts, commissions and bribes cover virtually every area of functioning and public interface, the integrity of public institutions has been seriously compromised and the working of the civil services affected at all levels. To achieve their short-term objectives, the political executive has been deploying pliant functionaries, handpicked on considerations of caste, community or political affiliations, to man key assignments.

Consequently, competence, integrity, experience and seniority are no longer relevant criteria for selecting the best officers to run the administrative structures, public sector enterprises and vital institutions. This has resulted in the cadres of the various civil services, including the police and judicial services, being demoralized and their functioning adversely affected. There are no role models any more since even persons of dubious distinction can get appointed to the highest posts in the country.

Sustained and systematic politicization has liquidated the command-and-control structures of the services, leading to indiscipline, inefficiency and unaccountability among the ranks. A growing number of employees in every sphere of functioning have amassed fortunes through corruption. Unseemly elements are accountable only to the politicians with whom they are aligned, their acts of omission and commission cannot be easily questioned by their superiors, who could possibly do so only at their own peril, considering the threatening environment in which the entire governmental system functions. In such a scenario, it is no wonder that the common man's woes go unheard; the image of the entire bureaucracy stands tarnished and there is justifiable criticism that nothing can be got done in any public office without bribing the functionaries concerned.

The poor, unemployed and disadvantaged segments of the population have no faith or trust in the ever expanding hierarchies which have been created to promote their welfare. The very sanctity and credibility of governance have been lost. It is well established that political influence and bribery are the most reliable route for any dealing with the administration.

As a result of the politicization of the administrative machinery, functionaries who are responsible for enforcing the law, for example the police, have got mixed up with the very elements whose unlawful activities they are expected to check and control. As the latter enjoy the patronage and protection of politicians, a frightening triangular nexus has evolved between criminals, government functionaries and politicians. That such a nexus had come into existence was brought out in a classified report prepared by the home secretary and submitted to the Union home minister in September 1993. Even though this report underlined the serious implications of the nexus for national security management, no tangible remedial action has materialized so far even though the Supreme Court had passed a clear direction regarding what was required to be done.

The Bofors scandal was exposed in 1987, soon followed by allegations of cut-backs having been received in the purchase of submarines from Germany. Thereafter many other scams have been unearthed, some of them involving embezzlement of thousands of crores. While investigations are reported to be under way in all such cases, and some of them have been put to trial, it is significant that so far none of the alleged offenders has been convicted. In fact, in several cases involving large-scale corruption, the accused have already been discharged. While it is for the higher courts to finally decide such cases, the perception among the public at large is that no corruption case involving persons in positions of influence (politicians, civil servants, bankers, technocrats, industrialists, etc.) can ever succeed for the simple reason that the state concerned and

Central investigation agencies have been so thoroughly politicized that strict investigations and a fair trial cannot take place. The CBI and CVC are the two principal agencies responsible for checking and dealing with corruption involving public servants. Unfortunately, their effectiveness and deterrence has long since been diluted.

For decades now, we have been engaging in intellectual debates, within and outside parliament, about the accountability of elected representatives in cases involving corruption, especially ministers, chief ministers and the prime minister. As this debate has not so far yielded the envisaged outcome, it has not been possible to introduce any worthwhile change in the ambit and provisions of the Prevention of Corruption Act or to promulgate a new and more effective law.

When the office of the CVC was originally established, it was expected that this organization would play a meaningful role in curbing dishonest functioning and check irregularities in the vast apparatus of the Central government and its public sector undertakings. When it was accepted – after the Supreme Court's ruling in the Hawala case – that the CVC had inadequate teeth, the incumbent of this office was given statutory status and specially empowered to overview the functioning of the CBI and the Enforcement Directorate of the Revenue Department. This was in 1998. However, due to the continuing political instability, this decision could not receive parliamentary approval and the office of the CVC stands reduced to its erstwhile status.

Well over three decades ago, a draft legislation, the Lokpal Bill, was mooted in parliament. Several expert groups and successive parliamentary standing committees have examined this bill in the past thirty years. Endless debates have taken place on whether an inquiry into allegations against the prime minister should be covered under the proposed law and the level up to which the bureaucracy should fall within its ambit. There has also been lack of agreement on the procedures and the safeguards which should cover the inquiries which may be ordered by the Lokpal. The bill remains pending and an effective legal framework under which the acts of corruption by public servants, up to the highest in the land, could be promptly gone into is still awaited.

The Prevention of Corruption Act continues to be in force but its ambit and application have been found inadequate to deal with corruption and misgovernance of senior-level bureaucracy and members of the elected executive. The working of this law has resulted in no more than junior and middle-level functionaries being convicted for resorting to dishonest practices. Even in cases in which investigations have been successfully concluded in major cases, offenders have escaped the dragnet because of indifferent and even prejudicial prosecution, prolonged delays in trials and the unwillingness of the competent courts to enforce their authority to bring such cases to a timely conclusion.

A consequence of the widespread corruption and unaccountability of our governance structures is that India stands high in the list of the 'most corrupt' countries and virtually at the bottom in international assessments of human development. This is partly due to the fact that even the funds for implementing vital poverty alleviation programmes are being embezzled. The Bihar fodder scam is an example of how development funds were looted under the personal direction of the highest authorities in the state. The annual reports of the Comptroller and Auditor General of India and the Public Accounts Committee (PAC) of parliament provide a bizarre picture of how public funds are being misused and embezzled virtually on a planned basis. The Supreme Court has passed strictures on several occasions in regard to the manner in which investigations were grossly delayed or misconducted in important cases involving allegations of corruption at the highest levels of government. Non-governmental organizations, social activist groups and the media have also been making valuable contributions in exposing cases of corruption in the states and at the Centre.

Despite heightened awareness of the incidence of corruption in public functioning, there is, as of now, no basis whatsoever to suggest that we are anywhere near controlling, much less eliminating, this cancerous growth in our body politic. This has most adversely affected the objectives of governance, from Delhi to the remotest village in the country. Recurring reports of billions of rupees being laundered or millions of rupees being seized in raids conducted by the enforcement agencies do not cause any special concern to the Cabinet or parliament. Such events appear to be taken as part of the game even though there are repeated pointers to how the existing malaise impacts on the security and the very integrity of the country.

It remains to be seen whether the new executive and parliament will muster the will to take urgent and effective steps to deal with the menace of corruption. If this were to happen, a bold view would have to be taken whether the rot, which is eating into the vitals of the nation, can be attributed only to the failings of a disintegrating bureaucracy. The time has come to introduce immediate reform of the electoral process and to honestly accept the role and culpability of politicians in positions of authority. No more than marginal results may accrue if it is decided merely to launch more stringent measures to cure the ailments of the bureaucracy, which is only a part of the total problem.

It would be foolhardy to forget that it is the responsibility of the elected executive to guide, direct and control the appointed executive. If the former continue with their short-term objective of thriving and surviving through corruption, we shall continue to have a dishonest, inefficient and unaccountable bureaucracy. This is likely to build a level of cynicism and despair which may compel the common man to seek the only remedy which lies within his means – a direct assault on those who represent the structures of authority. This would disrupt the established order and bring chaos in its wake.

Let us hope that those who have recently donned the mantle of governing our vast and populous country will have the courage and conviction to bring about the long-awaited reforms to clean up the sordid mess which presently envelops governance and establish clean and efficient systems which satisfy the people of India, are answerable to them, and take the country rapidly towards the attainment of its avowed goals.

17

Depoliticize Civil Services for a Better Tomorrow*

The Constitution of India provides the framework for the administration of the country through a uniform set of inter-related institutions. The Directive Principles of State Policy provide a non-justiciable foundation for a balanced and equitable socio-economic development. These principles are fundamental to the governance of the country, and the states are duty bound to follow them, enforcing the objectives through the enactment of necessary laws. The governance of the country is carried out through three vital instruments of the Constitution – the executive, legislature and judiciary.

Before attempting any prognosis of the kind of changes in the administrative apparatus which may be required to meet the challenges of the twenty-first century, it would be useful to at least rapidly review the experience so far of national governance.

The federal administrative system bequeathed by the British was largely continued after the attainment of Independence. Necessary changes to meet arising requirements were introduced in the subsequent years. The Indian Civil Service (ICS) and Indian Police (IP) were retained and legislation was enacted to create their successors: the Indian Administrative Service (IAS)

* First published in *The Tribune*, 15 August 1998.

and the Indian Police Service (IPS), and other required all-India Services (AIS).

The post-Independence challenges were complex, urgent and varied. The country faced a serious law and order situation. Hundreds of thousands of innocent persons were killed in the communal violence, rioting and arson which ravaged Punjab, Delhi, West Bengal and several other parts of the country. Besides the severe financial crunch, there was acute shortage of foodgrains and other essential supplies. Rationing was enforced and thousands of outlets for distributing food supplies had to be established to tackle the near-famine situation. Millions of refugees had to be provided food, shelter, clothing and medical care before setting upon the colossal task of rehabilitating them. All these and numerous other problems were most satisfactorily handled by the depleted administrative services in the provinces and at the Centre.

The first two decades after Independence witnessed significant progress on many fronts. The work done by the Planning Commission and the National Development Council laid the basis for the Centre and the states undertaking a collaborative endeavour for securing equitable socio-economic development and uplift of the poverty-stricken masses.

Consequent upon the humiliation faced in the 1962 Sino-Indian conflict, various measures were taken to strengthen the armed forces. The military regained its honour in the 1965 Indo-Pak engagement and earned fresh laurels in the 1971 Bangladesh war. Meanwhile, planned action had been taken to strengthen and enlarge the indigenous capability for meeting defence requirements and to connect the leaders with a network of roads and bridges. For improved border guarding and providing assistance to the states for internal security managements several new central police organizations were created – the ITBP, the BSF and the CISF.

All in all, till about the late 1960s, around the time the Congress started facing serious internal conflicts, the country seemed well set on the path of steady advancement. From then onwards governance in the states and the Centre started witnessing serious difficulties and consequent decline. A major factor for the deterioration has been the progressive loss of ideology and erosion of values among the political leadership.

Another factor which has had a deleterious effect on the much-needed evolution of a mature and stable polity is related to our election system. Over the years, there has been continuing increase in the number of political parties in all parts of the country.

In the last general elections, with well over 600 political parties participating in the polls, every seat was contested by far too many candidates. This has involved large-scale deployment of security forces and a huge increase in the governmental expenditure on the conduct of the polls. Another, and a far more serious consequence of such confusing electoral contests has been that in many states no single party has been able to secure a clear majority. Since 1996, formation of a government at the Centre has faced a similar serious situation.

The lack of necessary checks and balances in our electoral system has generated continuing political instability in the states and even at the Centre. To be able to lay claim to forming government, the party which gains the highest tally in the elections is compelled to garner the requisite majority by seeking the support of disparate small groups and even individuals, notwithstanding the sharp variations in the political ideologies and agendas, if any, of such elements. Such 'supporting' elements demand their pound of flesh on a daily basis, generating uncertainty about the longevity of the governments which they prop up.

A related and extremely worrying facet of our democratic process has been the large expenditure which a candidate has to bear for contesting a poll, especially if it relates to gaining a seat in the legislative assemblies or in parliament. While all political parties contesting elections collect funds through means fair or foul, to support their candidates, the parties in power in the states and at the Centre are more advantageously placed. They have, over the years, adopted the simple approach of exploiting their official positions to collect funds not only from trade, business and industry but from the public at large on almost every occasion that it requires to deal with the governmental machinery – allotments, auctions, registrations, grant of licences, recruitment to any service including the police, admissions to educational institutions, etc. The amounts collected generally relate to the degree of irregularity or illegality involved in the favour being done.

For example, if the existing customs regulations or excise or sales tax laws are compromised to specifically help the business interests of an Indian multinational, the rake-in may run into several billion rupees, some of which may be collected in foreign exchange in an undeclared foreign bank account (and this was the genesis of black money transactions and the 'hawala' business).

All such deviations from the norm are transacted through the officialdom; employees who quote rules or do not comply are promptly transferred and marginalized. Thus, over time, a strong nexus has grown between unprincipled politicians, pliant civil servants and the unseemly elements among those who perennially seek to support whichever political party is in power provided their unlawful demands are met.

Suffice it to say that the single-minded objective of political parties in power of retaining their position, brazenly indifferent to the misuse of authority, has led to their progressively identifying weak, compromising and aspiring elements in the civil, police and technical bureaucracies to subserve their unprincipled objectives. This has, over the years, led to the politicization of the cadres of the state services and even those which comprise the AIS, especially the IAS and IPS.

The extraordinary precedence given by the political masters to the 'committed' or 'loyal' elements in the various services has resulted in thoroughly undoing the laid-down principles, rules and regulations which govern recruitment, postings and appointments, tenures of field and secretarial posts, promotions, deputation for training at home or abroad et al. Officers who are not adequately malleable are transferred from post to post and station to station, in utter disregard of how this affects their training for handling higher responsibilities in due course, or how the repeated transfers of key functionaries disrupt the implementation of vital development programmes for which they are responsible, to say nothing about the effect on their morale and public esteem.

The rather frequent change of governments in some of the states has resulted in officers of various services, especially the collectors and superintendents of police, being shifted time and again. This vicious malady has got to a stage where appointments to key posts – especially those involving handling of large budgets, having dealings with industry and commerce, and the vital posts of district chiefs on the civil and police sides – are virtually put to auction. It would be puerile to expect that those who gain appointments on such terms of trade can even think of enforcing honesty, transparency and accountability in the areas of their respective functioning.

The disciplined and productive functioning of the cadres of various services in the states has been further vitiated by considerations of caste, community and ethnicity. The growth of regionalism and the increasing demand for greater autonomies for the states, alongside a growingly weaker Centre, have considerably reduced the strength of the Central authorities concerned in enforcing compliance by state governments of the statutory rules and regulations relating to the management of the AIS cadres. The unfettered manner in which the states have managed the Indian Administrative, Police and Forest Services has resulted in eroding the image and credibility of those who man them. Except issuing hapless advisories to the state governments, the Centre has been able to do no better than watch the continuing mismanagement of the AIS which, despite the serious constraints under which they operate, still provides vital support to the states and the Centre and help in holding the country together.

Failure of governance has generated a continuing debate and criticism. One view, often expressed, is that the existing failures in the functioning of the executive can be set right if the country shifts to a presidential form of government. Whatever may be done to make the functioning of the Centre more effective, we have to remain most seriously concerned about the quality of administration at the ground level, from which all our problems originate and some of which, due to sustained mismanagement, develop into national issues. Any change in the form of government at the Centre will not automatically result in curing the serious ailments in the administrative apparatus across the length and breadth of our vast country.

The government and parliament understand the need to enforce wide-ranging reforms in the continuing system of elections. After the wide publicity given to the criminal nexus report, mentioned earlier, there was a focused debate regarding the various measures required to at least keep persons with known criminal backgrounds out of the state legislatures and parliament. Even this limited objective has still to see fruition, to say nothing of the other important reforms required in the electoral process.

Against the backdrop of the continuing failures of the executive and the inability of a splintered parliament to provide the much needed direction, the judiciary has attempted to fill the yawning gaps in the governance of the country. While the recent phenomenon of 'judicial activism' generated considerable satisfaction among the public at large, it would be unwise to expect one of the instruments of the Constitution, which has a well-defined role, to take over the responsibilities of the executive and parliament and seek to remedy the failures of both. In any case, those who comprise the judiciary, executive and parliament are drawn from the same society.

However, much time and energy may be wasted if we embark upon any approach which assumes that mere structural changes in the administrative apparatus will result in improving the governance of this vast country of ours. We have spent the past several decades in negating the Constitution, abrogating the rule of law and systematically subverting the application of well-laid-down rules of government business and systems of functioning.

Let us spend the next few years in honestly and assiduously restoring the essentials of governance. There is no need to spend time and energy in thinking of inducting exotic concepts to restore good governance in the country. We have gained excellent experience in the entire field of development administration. We have highly competent and resourceful functionaries in all services, all over the country. All that we need to do is to ensure that such elements are provided recognition, the requisite security of tenures, and the opportunity of putting the system back on the rails. All those who cannot perform or are dishonest must be ruthlessly weeded out under whatever new legal framework which may be required to do this.

Appendixes

Appendix 1

Vohra Committee Report*
Ministry of Home Affairs

1.1   Government had (through its Order No.S/7937/SS(ISP)/93 dated 9th July '93) established a Committee, comprised as below, to take stock of all available information about the activities of crime Syndicates/Mafia organisations which had developed links with and were being protected by Government functionaries and political personalities. Based on the recommendations of the Committee, Government shall determine the need, if any, to establish a special organisation/agency to regularly collect information and pursue cases against such elements.

(i)	Home Secretary	Chairman
(ii)	Secretary (R)	Member
(iii)	DIB	Member
(iv)	Director CBI	Member
(v)	JS(PP) MHA	Member Secy.

1.2   The Committee was authorised to invite senior officers of various concerned Departments to gather the required information.

---

* Contained in 'RIGHT TO INFORMATION', published by Lok Shakti Abhiyan, JNU, New Delhi.

1.3   Special Secretary (Internal Security & Police), MHA, was subsequently added as a Member of the Committee. The Committee was desired to submit its Report within 3 months.

2.1   In the first meeting of the Committee (held on 15th July '93), I had explained to the Members that Government had established the Committee after seeing the reports of our Intelligence and Investigation agencies on the activities/ linkages of the Dawood Ibrahim gang, consequent to the bomb blasts in Bombay in March 1993. From these various reports, it was apparent that the activities of Memon Brothers and Dawood Ibrahim had progressed over the years, leading to the establishment of a powerful network. This could not have happened without these elements having been protected by the functionaries of the concerned Government departments, especially Customs, Income Tax, Police and others. It was, therefore, necessary to identify the linkages and to also determine how such information could be collected timely and acted upon in the future.

2.2   In the course of the discussions, I perceived that some of the Members appeared to have some hesitation in openly expressing their views and also seemed unconvinced that Government actually intended to pursue such matters. Accordingly, I addressed separate personal letters to each of the Members of the Committee seeking their well-considered suggestions and recommendations. Their responses are briefly brought out below.

SECRETARY (R&AW)

2.3   The various offices abroad of this Agency have limited strength and are largely geared to the collection of military, economic, scientific and political intelligence. R&AW monitors the activities of certain organisations abroad only insofar as they relate to their involvement with narco-terrorist elements and smuggling arms, ammunition, explosives, etc., into the country. It does not monitor the activities of criminal elements abroad, which are mainly confined to "normal smuggling without any links to terrorist elements". The present strength of the Agency's offices abroad would not permit it to enlarge its field of activities. If, however, there is evidence to suggest that these organisations have links with Intelligence agencies of other countries, particularly Pakistan, and that they are being used or are likely to be used by such countries for destabilising our economy, it would become R&AW's responsibility to monitor their activities, as is being done by this Agency to collect vital information in regard to the investigations in the Bombay bomb blasts case.

2.4   The creation of a nodal agency to collect information regarding the activities of Mafia organisations is very essential. All the existing information/data available with R&AW, IB and CBI could be made available to this nodal agency. R&AW will nominate an officer of suitable rank to liaise with the nodal agency on a regular basis to enable expeditious follow-up action.

DIRECTOR CBI

3.1   A Report on the nexus between the Bombay City Police and the Bombay underworld was prepared by CBI in 1986. It would be useful to institute a fresh study by CBI, on the basis of which appropriate administrative/legal measures could be initiated.

3.2   An organised crime Syndicate/Mafia generally commences its activities by indulging in petty crime at the local level, mostly relating to illicit distillation/gambling/organised satta and prostitution in the larger towns. In port towns, their activities involve smuggling and sale of imported goods and progressively graduate to narcotics and drug trafficking. In the bigger cities, the main source of income relates to real estate – forcibly occupying lands/buildings, procuring such properties at cheap rates by forcing out the existing occupants/tenants etc. Over time, the money power thus acquired is used for building up contacts with bureaucrats and politicians and expansion of activities with impunity. The money power is used to develop a network of muscle power which is also used by the politicians during elections.

3.3   CBI has reported that all over India crime Syndicates have become a law unto themselves. Even in the smaller towns and rural areas, musclemen have become the order of the day. Hired assassins have become a part of these organisations. The nexus between the criminal gangs, police, bureaucracy and politicians has come out clearly in various parts of the country. The existing criminal justice system, which was essentially designed to deal with the individual offences/crimes, is unable to deal with the activities of the Mafia; the provisions of law in regard to economic offences are weak; there are insurmountable legal difficulties in attaching/confiscation of the property acquired through Mafia activities.

3.4   It has been suggested that the menace has first to be tackled at the local level where the agencies of the State and the concerned Central Enforcement Agencies like Customs and Excise, Income Tax, etc., would be required to take effective action. In cases where a crime Syndicate has graduated to big business, it would be necessary to conduct detailed investigations into its assets, both movable and immovable. It has been stressed that when such action is not timely [sic] and effectively taken, the lower functionaries of the concerned State and Central Departments/organisations start over-looking the activities of the crime Syndicates. To elucidate this point, the Director CBI has given the example of IQBAL MIRCHI of Bombay who, till the late 1980s, was merely a visitor to passenger and carrier ships to obtain liquor and cigarettes for selling the same at a profit. In the last 3-4 years, MIRCHI acquired real estate valuing crores of rupees; he has many bank accounts and has been paying lakhs of rupees to his carriers. The growth of MIRCHI is due to the fact that the concerned Enforcement agencies did not take action in time against him and, later, this perhaps became difficult on account of the enormous patronage that he had developed. If MIRCHI is investigated, the entire patronage enjoyed by him and his linkages will come to light. Director CBI has observed that there are many such cases, such as that of MIRCHI, where the initial failure has led to the emergence of Mafia giants who have become too big to be tackled.

3.5   Director CBI has stated that the main mode of communications/contacts of the Mafias operating at the international level is through telephonic communications. Referring to the useful leads emerging from the investigations into the activities of Dawood Ibrahim, a Mafia leader, the Director CBI has stated that the effective monitoring of the telephone calls made from India/received from abroad would yield useful information and, for this to be done, Government may grant sanction to monitor certain telephone connections.

3.6   The assistance of Banks is an essential input. The Bank Managers can be placed under obligation to render reports on all heavy transactions and suspicious accounts to the Enforcement agencies. Such a practice obtains in UK.

3.7   Concluding his analysis, Director CBI has made the following suggestions to bring under control the activities of the criminal Syndicates:

(i)   Identification of offences and award of deterrent punishments, including preventive detention.

(ii)   Trial procedures should be simplified and hastened.

(iii) Surveillance should be carried out through fingerprinting, photographs and dossiers.

(iv) Monitoring mechanisms should be established at the State and Central levels.

(v) Establishment of Special Cells in the States CIDs and CBI.

(vi) Suitable amendments should be introduced in the existing laws to more effectively deal with the activities of Mafia organisations, etc.; this would also include review of the existing laws.

(vii) A detailed case study of 10–15 cases would provide useful information regarding the administrative/legal measures, which would be required to be taken to effectively tackle the functioning of Mafia organisations. The CBI can do this within a short period.

DIRECTOR, IB

6.1 DIB has reported that due to the progressive decline in the values of public life in the country, "warning signals of sinister linkage between the underworld politicians and the bureaucracy have been evident with disturbing regularity, as exemplified by the exposures of the networks of the Bombay blast case". He has recommended immediate attention to:

(i) Identification of the nexus between the criminals/ Mafias and anti-national elements on the one hand and bureaucrats, politicians and other sensitively located individuals on the other.

(ii) Identification of the nature and dimensions of these linkages and the modus operandi of their operations.

(iii) Assessment of the impact of these linkages on the various institutions, viz., the electoral, political, economic, law and order and the administrative apparatus.

(iv) Nexus, if any, between the domestic linkages with foreign intelligence.

(v) Necessary action to show effective action to counteract/ neutralise the Mafia activities.

(vi) Political and legal constraints in dealing with the covert/ illegal functioning of the linkages.

6.2 Like the Director CBI, the DIB has also stated that there has been a rapid spread and growth of criminal gangs, armed senas, drug Mafias, smuggling gangs, drug peddlers and economic lobbies in the country which have, over the years, developed an extensive network of contacts with the bureaucrats/ Government functionaries at the local levels, politicians, media persons and strategically located individuals in the non-State sector. Some of these Syndicates also have international linkages, including the foreign intelligence agencies. In this context, the DIB has given the following examples:

(i) In certain States, like Bihar, Haryana and UP, these gangs enjoy the patronage of local level politicians, cutting across party lines and the protection of governmental functionaries. Some political leaders become the leaders of these gangs/armed senas and, over the years, get themselves elected to local bodies, State Assemblies and the national Parliament. Resultantly, such elements have acquired considerable political clout, seriously jeopardizing the smooth functioning of the administration and the safety of life and property of the common man, causing a sense of despair and alienation among the people.

(ii) The big smuggling Syndicates, having international linkages, have spread into and infected the various economic and financial activities, including havala transactions, circulation of black money and operations of a vicious parallel economy causing serious damage to the economic fibre of the country. These Syndicates have acquired substantial financial and muscle power and social respectability and have successfully corrupted the government machinery at all levels and wield enough influence to make the task of Investigating and Prosecuting agencies extremely difficult; even the members of the Judicial system have not escaped the embrace of the Mafia.

(iii) Certain elements of the Mafia have shifted to narcotics, drugs and weapon smuggling and established narco-terrorism networks, specially in the States of J&K, Punjab, Gujarat and Maharashtra. The cost of contesting elections has thrown the politician into the lap of these elements and led to a grave compromise by officials of the preventive/detective systems. The virus has spread to almost all the centres in the country; the coastal and the border States have been particularly affected.

(iv) The Bombay bomb blast case and the communal riots in Surat and Ahmedabad have demonstrated how the Indian underworld has been exploited by the Pak ISI and the latter's network in UAE to cause sabotage, subversion and communal tension in various parts of the country. The investigations into the Bombay bomb blast cases have revealed extensive linkages of the underworld in the various governmental agencies, political circles, business sector and the film world.

6.3   DIB has stated that the network of the Mafia is virtually running a parallel Government, pushing the State apparatus into irrelevance. It is thus most immediately necessary that an institution is established to effectively deal with the menace. In this connection, the DIB has stated:

(i) Presently, there is no system/mechanism which is specifically designated to collect and collate intelligence pertaining to the linkages developed by crime Syndicates/Mafias with the governmental set up. Nonetheless, the various intelligence/investigation/enforcement agencies collect, in the normal course of their functioning, information about the nexus between the bureaucracy and politicians with the Mafia gangs, smugglers and the underworld. These agencies use such available inputs "only within the narrow confines of their work charter and choose not to take undue cognisance and follow-up action, leave alone sharing with any other agencies". Thus, all these agencies "function within their own cocoons, with the result that a plethora of information fails to get specific and purposeful attention needed for the exposure of the Linkages". It is therefore necessary to immediately have an institutionalised system which "while giving total freedom to the various agencies to pursue their charter of work, would simultaneously cast on them the onus of sharing such inputs to a nodal outfit whose job will be to process this information for attention of a single designated authority". This will enable the nodal Group to provide useful leads to the various agencies and, over time, a progressive database will get generated "to facilitate periodic reviews and analysis which could then be passed to a designated body".

7.1   As would be seen from the afore-stated brief discussion, especially the views expressed by Director CBI and DIB, it is evident that the muscle power of the crime Syndicates is sustained by their enormous financial power which, in turn, is secured by the Mafia elements by committing economic offences with impunity. In this context, I held detailed personal discussions with Secretary (Revenue) under whose control operate the various economic intelligence/investigative/enforcement agencies.

7.2   The Department of Revenue functions through the following major agencies:

(i)   Central Board of Excise & Customs (CBEC)

Inter alia, CBEC is responsible for the prevention of smuggling. In this and other tasks, it is assisted by the Director General of Revenue Intelligence (DGRI) and the Directorate General of Anti-Evasion (DGAE). The DGRI deals with the evasion of customs duties; the DGAE with Excise duty evasion.

(ii)   Central Board of Direct Taxes (CBDT)

Income Tax Department administers the Income Tax Act, Wealth Tax Act, etc.

(iii) Central Economic Intelligence Bureau (CEIB)

The CEIB is responsible for coordinating and strengthening the intelligence gathering activities and the investigative and enforcement actions of the various agencies responsible for investigation into economic offences and the enforcement of economic laws. The CEIB is responsible for maintaining liaison with the concerned Departments/Directorates both at the Centre and at the State levels and is expected to provide overall direction to the investigative agencies under the Department of Revenue.

The CEIB is expected, inter alia, to attend to the following tasks:

(a) Identification of major sources generating black money; directing and developing intelligence about such sources; planning and coordinating action and operations against such sources.

(b) Assisting the various enforcement agencies in strengthening the intelligence gathering infrastructure and building up their capability for storage and retrieval of intelligence.

(c) Conducting investigative and analytical studies in difficult areas of black money operations and monitoring indicators thereof.

(iv) Enforcement Directorate

This Directorate is concerned with the enforcement of the investigation and penal provision of the Foreign Exchange Regulation Act; collection of intelligence relating to foreign exchange offences; enquiries into suspected violations of the provisions of FERA, etc.

(v) Narcotics Control Bureau (NCB)

The NCB is responsible for the administration of the Narcotic Drugs and Psychotropic Substances Act. It is responsible for coordination with different Central and State Government Departments/Ministries and the various Central and State law enforcement agencies for the implementation of the NDPS Act.

7.3 I explained to Secretary (Revenue) the broad considerations on account of which the government had set up a Committee to look into the linkages developed by the Mafia elements. He informed me that he had recently held a meeting with senior representatives of the RBI, the Chairman CBEC, Chairman CBDT and the Economic Intelligence Council in the Department of Revenue, and readily agreed with my request to attend a meeting of the Committee along with his concerned officers for a full discussion on the issues before the Committee. Accordingly, I arranged a meeting of the Committee (30th Aug '93) to hear the views of Secretary (Revenue), who was accompanied by chairman CBDT, DGRI, Member (Customs) and Director (Enforcement). During the course of the discussions with Secretary (Revenue) and his aforesaid principal officers, the following significant observations were made:

(i) In the normal course of his work, to detect violations of Customs & Excise laws, the DGRI comes across information on linkages [between] crime Syndicates and governmental functionaries etc. As following of such information is not within the charter of duties of

DGRI, his officers focus primarily on the information relating to the violation of laws relating to their charter.

(ii) As in the case of DGRI, indirect information also becomes available [with] the CBDT about linkages. Here again, not being directly related to their charter of responsibilities, the CBDT does not follow up on such leads.

(iii) While the NCB is specifically responsible for booking drug traffickers, with increasing importance being given to Narco-terrorism, the NCB has been asked to gather further information so that the real kingpins in the narcotics trade can be apprehended.

(iv) The Directorate of Enforcement comes across information on linkages and passes it on to the CBI and IB.

(v) Of late, currency amounting to crores of rupees is being seized, invariably packed in suitcases and gunny bags. The Banks are reluctant to pass on information about account holders to CBDT and do not allow their officers to hold exploratory enquiries.

(vi) While a certain amount of information is shared between the various organisations under the Department of Revenue, and those under the MHA and Cabinet Secretariat, the exchanges are sporadic and limited. This is perhaps due to the fact that each concerned organisation/agency is anxious to protect its sources and is apprehensive that a full sharing of all information might jeopardise its operations, on account of premature leakage of information.

(vii) While DGRI, Director (Enforcement) and DG NCB are authorised to undertake phone tapping of suspected offenders, the DGRI has not been allowed to enforce surveillance on the telephonic communications of political personalities.

(viii) Senior Police officers, even in the border States, are not trained or adequately informed of the work done by the Directorate of Enforcement, specially in regard to money laundering operations.

(ix) Information about the activities of drug traffickers is passed on by DG NCB to the concerned State Governments and their agencies. However, niggardly responses by the latter and prolonged delays in the disposal of cases before the Courts seriously hampers the effective functioning of the NCB. While the NDPS Act prescribes the award of deterrent punishments to offenders, the results are to the contrary. It is necessary that the Directorates of Prosecution in the State Governments are urgently brought under the control of the State Police.

...

7.5   Secretary (Revenue) stated that the field officers of his various Departments were faced with various problems, amongst which are:

(i)   The utter inadequacy of the criminal justice system; cases are not heard in time; functioning of the Government lawyers is grossly inadequate; all this results in a low percentage of convictions and mild punishments. Unless the criminal justice system is geared up, the work of the enforcement agencies cannot be effective.

(ii)   The field officers of the various agencies of the Revenue Department are often pressurised by senior government functionaries/political leaders, apparently at the behest of crime Syndicates/Mafia elements. Unless the field level officers are offered effective protection, they cannot be expected to maintain interest in vigorously pursuing action against the activities of such elements.

7.6   Chairman CBDT stated that insofar as the functioning of his officers is concerned, whenever they come into possession of any information regarding the violation of any other law, they pass it on to the concerned agency. He suggested that if the information available with other agencies is passed on to him, his officers could pursue the same.

8.1   As a result of the discussions held by the Committee with Secretary (Revenue) and his principal officers, it is evident that:

(i)   while, in the course of their normal activities, information on the linkages of the crime Syndicates sometimes becomes available, such information is not pursued on the score that it is not directly related to offences falling within the laws administered by these agencies;

(ii)   such information is occasionally passed on by these agencies to the CBI and or IB;

(iii)   the various agencies under the Department of Revenue do not specifically search out information on the linkages of crime Syndicates.

9.1   Consequent to the Committee's discussions with the Secretary (Revenue) and his principal officers, I held a series of further personal discussions with the Secretary (Revenue). At my request, Secretary (Revenue) gave me a personal note indicating his views, which are briefly as below:

(i)   The information gathered by the various agencies under the Revenue Department, while gathering intelligence on offences relating to the laws administered by them, is generally not put to any use unless it is required to be passed on to other intelligence agencies outside the Department of Revenue.

(ii)   The linkages developed by crime Syndicates get generally confirmed when pressure is mounted on the concerned agencies not to take action against the offenders or to go slow in the cases against them. Such pressures are mounted either immediately after a raid is conducted or at the time when prosecution is about to be initiated. Pressures are also exerted whenever corrupt and undesirable officers are shifted from sensitive assignments (Preventive Customs Divisions at the Airports, sensitive Collectorates in the Central Excise, etc.).

(iii) In the narcotics arena, which includes cultivation of opium, manufacture of alkaloids, prevention of narcotics, smuggling, etc., the financial stakes are astronomically high. Consequently, the level of corruption is of a very high order in this area of functioning and enormous pressures are brought to bear even when subordinate officials are posted away especially when the shift of an officer adversely affects the interests of those who are making easy money.

(iv) Narcotics trade has a worldwide network of smugglers who also have close links with terrorists. Terrorists indulge in narcotics trade to amass huge funds, in various foreign currencies, from which they source their weapons, etc.

9.2   While the Department of Revenue has initiated a number of steps to deal with the activities of smugglers and to plug loopholes in the system, Secretary (Revenue) has stated that a possible approach to effectively liquidating the linkages developed by the crime Syndicates would be to mercilessly prosecute the offenders without succumbing to any pressure whatsoever. He is of the view that once the offenders are deterrently [sic] punished under the law, their influence and strength will start declining, as also of all those who support them, wherever located. He has emphasised that for this objective to be achieved, it will be extremely necessary that: the entire governmental machinery involved in taking action against the crime Syndicates is allowed to perform its duties with total freedom; officers with impeccable integrity should be posted to head the various organisations which are responsible for taking action against tax offenders, smugglers, etc.; such officers should be selected with utmost care and provided sufficiently long tenures, giving them the clear mandate to ruthlessly punish the offenders; action must be taken to ensure the objective functioning of Courts which deal with the trial of economic offences; all cases before the Courts should be speedily concluded without the judicial officers coming under any pressure or succumbing to temptations; inefficient and corrupt elements in the various organisations must be weeded out and Government should take stringent action against officers who seek to exert political pressure for securing postings and appointments of their choice.

10.1　From the above narrated analysis, the following conclusions can be drawn:

(i)　On the basis of the extensive experience gained by our various concerned intelligence, investigative and enforcement agencies, it is apparent that crime Syndicates and Mafia organisations have established themselves in various parts of the country.

(ii)　The various crime Syndicates /Mafia organisations have developed significant muscle and money power and established linkages with governmental functionaries, political leaders and others to be able to operate with impunity (as recently exemplified by the activities of the Memon Brothers and Dawood Ibrahim).

(iii)　While the CBI and IB and the various agencies under the Department of Revenue, in their normal course of functioning, come across information relating to the linkages of crime Syndicates/Mafia organisations, there is presently no system under which they are expected to pass on such information to an identified nodal agency.

Sharing of such information is presently of an occasional nature and no evidence is available of the same having been put to any operational use (the only mentionable exception perhaps relates to the recent investigations into the activities of Memon Brothers and the Dawood gang on which several of our agencies were put to work collectively).

11.1 Even where an agency comes across certain information about the linkages of crime Syndicates, it has no mandate to immediately pass it on to one or more agencies. An agency which comes across information regarding linkages is also apprehensive that the sharing of such information may jeopardise its own functioning through premature leakage. In sum, the various agencies presently in the field take care to essentially focus on their respective charter of duties, dealing with the infringement of laws relating to their organisations and consciously putting aside any information on linkages which they may come across.

12.1 In the discussions in the Committee, I asked each of the Members as well as the Secretary (Revenue) and his principal officers about their views regarding the establishment of a Nodal Agency for the collection, collation and operationalisation of all information relating to the activities of crime Syndicates. Broadly, the following approaches have been mooted:

(i) The DIB has stated that while considering the establishment of any nodal mechanism, "it must be appreciated that the problems has enormous impact on national security and is indeed highly political in nature". In this context, he has suggested that the nodal set up should be under the IB, which is even otherwise engaged in monitoring various political activities having a bearing on national security. He has recommended that "an exclusive Top Secret Cell be established in the IB to function as the Nodal Group for receipt of inputs from various security/revenue agencies which reveal a politician–bureaucrat–underworld nexus. Such sharing will be through personal communications in writing, while operating difficulties could be sorted out through periodic meetings among the heads of these organisations to be chaired by the Home Secretary."The Top Secret Cell will share all tactical and operational information with other concerned agencies on "need to know and act basis".

(ii) The other approach recommended is to set up a system under which the Heads of the various Intelligence and Revenue agencies shall meet on a regular basis and exchange vital information, without there being any leakage.

13.1 In the background of the discussions so far, there does not appear to be need for any further debate on the vital importance of setting up a nodal point to which all existing intelligence and Enforcement agencies (irrespective of the Department under which they are located) shall promptly pass on any information which they may come across, which relates to the activities of crime Syndicates.

13.2 If the preposition in the preceding para is sustained, a decision will need to be taken regarding the Department/ Ministry under which the nodal set-up should be located.

14.1 Under the existing arrangements for the transaction of Government business, the Ministry of Home Affairs is responsible for all matters relating to internal security. It is for this reason that the Intelligence Bureau is a part and parcel of this Ministry (It is only by tradition that the DIB reports directly to authorities outside MHA). R&AW functions under the Cabinet Secretariat and deals with external intelligence. The various Intelligence, Investigation and Enforcement agencies dealing with the implementation of economic laws report to the Revenue Department under the Ministry of Finance. The CBI, which is the principal criminal investigation agency of the Centre, is under the Department of Personnel.

14.2   In my view, considerable care would have to be taken to ensure that the information which becomes available to the Nodal Cell is handled by a very senior and trust-worthy officer. Any leakage of such information would not only jeopardise potential action against the powerful criminal Syndicates, but may also be susceptible to political exploitation. Under all circumstances, it will have to be ensured that the information available with the nodal set-up is used strictly and entirely for stringent action against the crime Syndicates, without allowing any scope whatever of its being exploited for political gain.

14.3   In the preceding context, it would be logical if the nodal set-up is under the MHA, directly handled by the Home Secretary who can be assisted by one or more selected officers of the Ministry for the collation and compilation of all information received from IB, CBI, R&AW and the various agencies under the Department of Revenue The manner in which such information is operationalised would need to be confidentially discussed with the concerned Heads of Organisations and, as necessary, with Secretary (Revenue). It will also need to be ensured that the nodal set-up functions with extreme secrecy. Needless to say, any leakage whatever about the linkages of crime syndicate, senior Government functionaries or political leaders in the states or at the Centre could have a destabilizing effect on the functioning of Government. As such, it would not appear prudent to entrust the functioning of the Nodal Cell to any level below that of the Home Secretary. Further, the government would also have to carefully consider and prescribe the authorities to whom the Home Secretary will report in regard to the sensitive information received by the nodal set-up as well as regarding the operations to be launched by one or more of the concerned agencies to apprehend, investigate and prosecute the offenders.

15.1   In the normal course this report would have been drafted by the Mernber Secretary and finalised by the Committee. Considering the nature of the issues involved, I did not consider it desirable to burden the Members of the Committee with any further involvement beyond the views expressed by them. Accordingly, I decided to personally dictate this Report.

15.2   I have prepared only three copies of this Report. One copy each is being submitted to MOS(IS) and HM, the third copy being retained by me. After HM has perused this Report, I request him to consider discussing further action with finance minister, MOS(IS) and myself. The emerging approach could thereafter be got approved from Prime Minister before being implemented. At that stage other concerned senior officers would be taken into confidence.

15.3   After an initial discussion at the level of MOS(IS) and HM I could send a copy of this Report to FM, before the issues are discussed with him.

Sd/-

(N. N. Vohra)
Home Secretary
5.10.93

Appendix 2

Lessons from Purulia*

The recent para-dropping of lethal munitions by a foreign aircraft in certain villages of West Bengal reminds us, yet again, that the internal security management of our country is far from satisfactory. This incident also reminds us that external and internal security issues are seriously intermeshed and there must be total clarity in regard to the respective roles and responsibilities of the defence forces and all the civilian authorities involved in national security.

It has been reported that a foreign AN-26 transport aircraft was flying from Karachi to Yangon and had the clearance of the Directorate General of Civil Aviation (DGCA) to overfly Indian territory with permission to halt at Varanasi and Calcutta. The aircraft stopped at Varanasi for refuelling. The DGCA personnel here did not examine the relevant documents, much less attempt to even randomly inspect the cargo on board the aircraft. From Varanasi the aircraft took an excessively long period of two hours to reach Calcutta, where also the concerned staff asked no questions about the journey time and undertook no checking of the documents, log books or the cargo. The crew happily stayed for the night in Calcutta!

Meanwhile, there was accidental detection of the lethal cargo, which had been dropped in one of the villages in Purulia district.

---

* First published in *The Indian Express*, 1 January 1996.

Certain initial reports on this grave incident suggested that the episode was perhaps attributable to a misadventure by an Indian intelligence agency! Emboldened by his experience at Varanasi and Calcutta, the pilot took further liberties on the return journey to Pakistan. The aircraft landed at Madras without the required DGCA clearance. It was only after the aircraft took off from Madras that an alarm was sounded and two Indian Air Force (IAF) planes forced it to land at Bombay. Despite the serious circumstances which led to IAF's involvement, the Bombay staff was unprepared to deal with the situation and the co-pilot was allowed to slip away. He is still to be arrested.

It has also been reported that the AN-26 had a 'dry run' before actually paradropping its cargo in Purulia and that a Central intelligence agency had provided advance information about the possibility of weapons and ammunition being airdropped in the country. It has even been suspected that this or other aircraft may have been happily running similar missions into our country in the past and that the AN-26 had offloaded part of its cargo at some other site, besides the paradropping in Purulia.

After the repeated failure in regard to the AN-26, the DGCA seems to have become overactive and, in quick succession, another AN-26 was forced down at Delhi and a civilian jet aircraft travelling from Muscat to China was almost compelled to force-land by the IAF. In the latter case, neither the Ahmedabad nor the Bombay Air Traffic Controls (ATCs) had prior information about the designated flight path of this aircraft or about the DGCA clearance it possessed.

The Central intelligence agencies have known, at least since the 1980s, of the ISI's well-organized efforts to destabilize our frontier states by inducting trained persons and weaponry across our land borders to foment fundamentalism and insurgency. The Punjab situation has still to be brought fully under control and that in Jammu and Kashmir (J&K) and the north-eastern states is a cause for continuing concern. With our security forces revamping their presence on our northern and western land borders, the ISI had resorted to coastal intrusions. The bomb blasts in Bombay in early 1993 revealed that weaponry and other instruments of destruction had been inducted into the country along the western coast. Against this background, it should not have been beyond the imagination of the intelligence agencies that our adversary would also explore every possible means of airdropping munitions in selected areas.

In the past few years there has been considerable increase in civil aviation traffic due to the growth of private airlines and new link-ups with foreign countries. Thus, today, the Indian airspace is intensively utilized by a variety of aircraft owned and run by various Indian agencies and by aircraft of foreign origin.

The Ministry of Civil Aviation and its various agencies, especially the DGCA, are responsible for taking all necessary measures and effectively enforcing them to ensure that no civil aircraft overflies our territory or lands at our ports without due scrutiny of the source of the request, the nature of aircraft being flown from where to where, carrying whom or what, etc. Permits issued by the DGCA to foreign aircraft to overfly and/or land/ refuel stipulate well-defined steps to be followed in each case and, if a landing is allowed, the nature of scrutiny to which the crew, passengers and cargo are to be subjected.

The stipulations enforced by the DGCA have a twin objective: to ensure the safety of movement of various kinds of aircraft criss-crossing our skies and, equally important, to ensure national security interests. Once a valid permit is issued for overflying Indian territory and/or landing at Indian airports, it is the responsibility of the DGCA to ensure that its officials meticulously carry out the checks. It is apparent that the AN-26 did not encounter any inspection or questioning at all during its forward flight and, on its return journey, wantonly proceeded to Madras from where also it managed to get through. If the DGCA systems had worked, the aircraft and its crew would have been subjected to a thorough inspection at Varanasi and taken into custody.

In any case, after leaving Varanasi, the ATCs at both Varanasi and Calcutta should have monitored its movement. If the pilot consciously broke radio contact, a search alarm should have been sounded and the IAF informed immediately. The defence radars do not have unlimited area surveillance; they focus on point-to-point coverage for their own reasons. Thus, technically, unless the DGCA informs the IAF about the unauthorised entry of a civil aircraft in our airspace, the latter would virtually remain uninformed. In this context, for safeguarding national security, it is imperative that the DGCA pass on real-time information to IAF within seconds of any suspected intrusion. Ideally, the civil and military radar systems should be interlinked and operate in a network, at least in the vulnerable sectors.

Given the security scenario which has obtained in our country for the last fifteen years, the Purulia incident denotes failure of a nature which belies categorization. If it is true that one of the Central agencies had prior information about the possibility of such an attempt being made, there was gross failure to provide the available intelligence to all concerned, especially to the DGCA.

This case would suggest that those responsible have not so far had any occasion to even realize the vital importance of ensuring flawless civil aviation security management to support national air defence. Entrusting further inquiries to the CBI and setting up inter-ministerial coordination committees may, for the moment, appear steps in the right direction. Experience has, however, abundantly shown that national security goals cannot be adequately secured unless areas of responsibility are clearly demarcated and accountability ruthlessly enforced.

Let us hope that the Purulia incident will compel the Central authorities to undertake a comprehensive review of the national security apparatus and enforce prompt, effective and accountable performance by each of the agencies involved. Unless this is done most urgently grave dangers lie ahead.

About the Author

N.N. Vohra has been the Governor of Jammu and Kashmir since 2008. Educated at Punjab and Oxford Universities, he was in the Indian Administrative Service (1959–94) and served as Secretary, Defence Production, Defence Secretary and Home Secretary. Post retirement, he was recalled to serve as Principal Secretary to Prime Minister (1997–98).

After superannuation, he served as member of the first National Security Advisory Board (1998–2001) and headed the National Task Force on Internal Security (2000). He was founder co-chair of the India–European Union Round Table (2001–08) and served as Director, India International Centre, New Delhi, for over eight years.

He was awarded the Paul H. Appleby Award (2014) for his meritorious work in the field of public administration and received the Padma Vibhushan (2007) for his long years of distinguished service to the nation.